NOV – 2007

CIVILIZATION
AND ITS
DISCONTENTS

By SIGMUND FREUD

AN AUTOBIOGRAPHICAL STUDY
BEYOND THE PLEASURE PRINCIPLE
CIVILIZATION AND ITS DISCONTENTS
THE COMPLETE INTRODUCTORY LECTURES ON PSYCHOANALYSIS
THE EGO AND THE ID
FIVE LECTURES ON PSYCHOANALYSIS
THE FUTURE OF AN ILLUSION
GROUP PSYCHOLOGY AND THE ANALYSIS OF THE EGO
INHIBITIONS, SYMPTOMS AND ANXIETY
INTRODUCTORY LECTURES ON PSYCHOANALYSIS
JOKES AND THEIR RELATION TO THE UNCONSCIOUS
LEONARDO DA VINCI AND A MEMORY OF HIS CHILDHOOD
NEW INTRODUCTORY LECTURES ON PSYCHOANALYSIS
ON DREAMS
ON THE HISTORY OF THE PSYCHOANALYTIC MOVEMENT
AN OUTLINE OF PSYCHOANALYSIS
THE PSYCHOPATHOLOGY OF EVERYDAY LIFE
THE QUESTION OF LAY ANALYSIS
TOTEM AND TABOO

THE STANDARD EDITION
OF THE COMPLETE PSYCHOLOGICAL WORKS OF
SIGMUND FREUD
24 VOLUMES

W. W. NORTON & COMPANY

New York / London

SIGMUND FREUD

CIVILIZATION AND ITS DISCONTENTS

INTRODUCTION BY
Louis Menand

TRANSLATED AND EDITED BY
James Strachey

BIOGRAPHICAL AFTERWORD BY
Peter Gay

Copyright © 1961 by James Strachey
Copyright © 1989 by Peter Gay
Copyright © 2005 by Louis Menand

Illustration by Gustave Dore, *Fallen Angels* / Corbis

All rights reserved
Printed in the United States of America

For information about permission to reproduce selections from this book, write to
Permissions, W. W. Norton & Company, Inc., 500 Fifth Avenue, New York, NY 10110

Manufacturing by Quebecor World, Fairfield
Book design by Jo Anne Metsch
Production manager: Amanda Morrison

Library of Congress Cataloging-in-Publication Data

Freud, Sigmund, 1856-1939.
[Unbehagen in der Kultur. English]
Civilization and its discontents / Sigmund Freud; introduction by Louis Menand; translated
and edited by James Strachey; biographical afterword by Peter Gay.
p. cm.
Includes bibliographical references and index.
ISBN 0-393-05995-2 (hardcover)
1. Psychoanalysis. 2. Civilization. I. Strachey, James. II. Title.
BF173.F682 2005
150.19'52—dc22
2004027112

W. W. Norton & Company, Inc., 500 Fifth Avenue, New York, N.Y. 10110
www.wwnorton.com

W. W. Norton & Company Ltd., Castle House, 75/76 Wells Street, London W1T 3QT

1 2 3 4 5 6 7 8 9 0

CONTENTS

INTRODUCTION

by Louis Menand

Sigmund Freud's *Civilization and Its Discontents* is in a class with Plato's *Republic*, Milton's *Paradise Lost*, Marx's *Capital*, and Hegel's *Phenomenology of Spirit*: the grounds have entirely eroded for whatever authority it once enjoyed as an ultimate account of the way things are, but we can no longer understand the way things are without taking it into account. Like the Commendatore in Mozart's *Don Giovanni*, its afterlife is in certain respects more impressive than its life, and for the same reason. It can no longer be killed.

Students of Freud divide his career into two phases, the first dating from the publication of *The Interpretation of Dreams*, in 1899, and the second from the time of the First World War. The second phase was revisionist: Freud changed his mind about many of the concepts on which the discipline of psychoanalysis had been established, and he created what is essentially a new system. Freud's reasons for retooling, beyond the one that he gave, which is that the earlier system had logical inconsistencies, are obscure. The hardships and horrors of the War might have been an impetus; Freud's desire to preserve his standing as the leader of his own movement is a possibility that it would be imprudent to discount. Freud's earlier system is usually referred to as "topographical," the later one as "structural." But to people who are not analysts, the technical distinction will seem less important than the general change in focus, and they will find it more useful to say what Freud himself said, which is that at a certain point in his career, he turned his attention from the problems of the individual to the problems of culture.

This interest produced *Totem and Taboo* (1913), *Group Psychology and the Analysis of the Ego* (1921), *The Future of an Illusion* (1927), and *Moses and Monotheism* (1937). *Civilization and Its Discontents* is its key text. Freud wrote it when he was seventy-three and already suffering from the cancer of the jaw that eventually killed him, after a lifetime of cigar smoking (a habit which he analyzed as a substitute for "the primal addiction," masturbation). The book was finished in 1929 and published in early 1930, a few months after the New York stock market crashed. It was the most popular of Freud's books; a second printing, in 1931, allowed him to add a new final sentence, which apparently alludes to the Nazi Party's success in the German elections in September 1930. Freud died, in 1939, in Hampstead, a refugee from the Nazis. (Fifty-six years before, Karl Marx had died in Hampstead, a refugee from a different German regime.)

Although Freud obviously had no notion of the Holocaust or Hiroshima when he wrote it, *Civilization and Its Discontents* came to be read, after 1945, as a comment on what those events seemed to reveal about human nature and human possibility. It became a staple of cold war thought, and it inspired conservatives as well as radicals—something that would not have surprised its author, who believed that an incorrigible feature of all affective dispositions, love as well as hate, is ambivalence.

Civilization and Its Discontents is not a work of literature. It is not a work of philosophy, either. It is a work of scientific speculation, and although everyone can deal with the speculative part, not everyone is happy with the science. It's a mistake to ignore it, though. When Freud is attacked for being unscientific, his admirers sometimes suggest that his theories should be taken heuristically and metaphorically—as pictures and parables of mental life, verified by the aid they give to understanding and to the relief of suffering, in the way that the truth of a poem or a painting is verified by the purchase it gives us on life, rather than by its literal correspondence to reality. Freud did occasionally drop hints that this was the spirit in which he ought to be read. "Though I have the appearance of a scientist I was and am a poet and novelist," he told the Italian writer Giovanni Papini in 1934. "Psychoanalysis is no more than the interpretation of a literary vocation in terms of psychology and pathology." But remarks like this are far outnumbered by the claims, made repeatedly by Freud and his epigones, for the scientific bona fides of psychoanalysis. Freud liked to say that his ideas were anticipated by the poets, but he did not mean that poetry was their sole corroboration. He was trained as a medical scientist, and all of his theories arose out of his attempt to deal with what nineteenth-century Western science regarded as a medical problem. The problem was hysteria.

Hysteria is a condition historically associated with women; the term derives from the Greek word for womb. In 1868, the American physician George Beard identified a type of hysteria in men—he called it "neurasthenia"—and (as has been known to happen) the suggestion that men were susceptible to an affliction once believed restricted to women enhanced its appeal as a target for research. The reason hysteria is a problem is somatization. The hysteric has bodily symptoms, which may range from migraines to paralysis of the limbs. (Henry James's sister, Alice, suffered from both.) But efforts to locate the physical causes of these symptoms, such as lesions in the brain, or to undertake conventional medical interventions, such as drugs or electric shock, were ineffective. When he was a young man, Freud was a student of the most prominent researcher on hysteria in the world, Jean Martin Charcot, and one of the things he learned from Charcot was that psychiatric techniques, specifically, hypnotism, got better results than did medication or orders to snap out of it (a common treatment in the nineteenth century, later used, without success, by General George Patton). Most nineteenth-century scientists believed that the mind, or consciousness, is wholly conditioned by the physical brain: they regarded every mental experience as the effect of some organic cause. The hysteric's "conversion" (the clinical term) of psychic distress into physical symptoms enabled Freud to flip this assumption on its head. Psychoanalysis is an attempt to treat nervous disorders as basically mental rather than basically physical. As one historian, Frank Sulloway, has put it, Freud was the first biologist of the mind.

Freudian theory is therefore embedded in the assumptions of nineteenth-century biology. One of these assumptions is recapitulation, the so-called biogenetic law—the belief that the development of the individual (ontogeny) recapitulates the evolution of the species (phylogeny). Recapitulation means that as the human fetus grows, it passes through stages in which it resembles the life-forms, from single-cell organisms onwards, from which the human species evolved. Another assumption is Lamarckianism—the belief that acquired characteristics can be inherited. Lamarckianism means that the course of evolution can be affected by changes in the environment, which may alter the genetic material that shapes the next generation. If the giraffe stretches its neck to reach the leaves higher up on the tree, its offspring will be born with longer necks; if people go to school and work to become smarter, they can pass along better "smartness" genes to their children.

Most recapitulationists and Lamarckians believed in the perfectibility of the species; for those theories suggest that nature evolves progressively, from lower to higher forms, and that it is possible for advances in civilization to produce advances in human types—that we can "lift up" the race. Darwin's theory of evolution by natural selection was not a theory of perfectibility. Natural selection operates by chance, and its bottom line is survival for the purpose of reproduction, and by whatever means necessary, good, bad, or ugly. It's about life going onward but not, necessarily, upward. Darwin was one of Freud's heroes, and although Freud believed in the biogenetic law and the inheritability of acquired characteristics, notions that are peripheral to Darwinism, he distinctly did not believe in the perfectibility of the human race. *Civilization and Its Discontents* was written to explain why.

When he set out to analyze culture (*Kultur*, not *Zivilisation*, is the word that Freud used in his book; the distinction is significant), Freud did what he had done thirty years before, when he set out to analyze hysteria as a physical response to mental experiences: he reversed the accepted sequence of cause and effect. Most people assume that individuals are shaped by the society in which they're raised. Freud thought that it was the other way around, that society is just a macro form of the individual, and takes its imprint from individual psychology. "The events of human history . . . are only the reflections of the dynamic conflicts among the ego, id, and superego, which psychoanalysis studies in the individual—the same events repeated on a wider stage," he explained in *The Future of an Illusion*. This was the logic of recapitulation. It allowed Freud to read back from the etiology of his patients' neuroses to the ori-

gins of human culture—since, under the provisions of the biogenetic law, the development of the individual repeats development of the race. "It seems to me a most surprising
discovery," he explained in *Totem and Taboo*, "that the problems
of social psychology . . . should prove soluble on the basis of a
single concrete point—man's relation to his father," which is,
of course, precisely the basis on which the problems of personal psychology prove soluble according to psychoanalysis.
Religion, morals, society, and art, Freud claimed, all originate
in the Oedipus complex. Civilization began when the young
men of the tribe ganged up and murdered the father-figure, the
tribal leader who had appropriated all the women for his own
sexual use. The guilt they experienced (since hatred is ambiva-
lent: they loved their leader, too) is the origin of the *Über-Ich*—
the superego—and of the repression that makes culture
possible.

Later on, needless to say, sons do not actually murder their
fathers for refusing to share the sexual favors of their mothers
(although they supposedly wish to do so when they are in the
oedipal stage of development). But they continue to feel the
primal guilt that traumatized the ancestors who actually committed that crime—a theory made possible by Lamarckianism:
guilt is an acquired characteristic that got passed along. In *Civilization and Its Discontents*, Freud analyzed guilt and the feelings
of anxiety and depression that accompany it—moods that we
get into even when we know that we have no real reason to be

in them—as the repression of the aggressive impulse. We suffer from guilt, anxiety, and depression because we have turned the impulse to kill the father inwards, on ourselves. We have done nothing wrong; even our wish to do something wrong is preconscious. But we continue to punish ourselves because once upon a time, men lacked conscience. After *Civilization and Its Discontents* came out, Freud told a group of colleagues that the analysis of guilt as displaced aggression was the book's central idea, and, he said, "the most important progress" in psychoanalysis. He was, in part, defending against the complaint that he had written *Civilization and Its Discontents* in order to introduce the concept of the death-drive into psychoanalysis.

The death-drive is a difficult concept that has been made more difficult by terminological confusion. The peculiarity of the English translations used for the Standard Edition of Freud's works, which were overseen by James Strachey and Freud's daughter Anna, is the subject of a substantial literature. Bruno Bettelheim wrote a whole book about it. The term Freud used for the death-drive was *Todestrieb*. Strachey chose to render *Trieb*, throughout the Standard Edition, as "instinct" rather than "drive," a word, he insisted, that does not exist with Freud's meaning in English. But as Strachey conceded, Freud did use the word *Instinkt*, and he used it almost exclusively to refer to patterns of behavior in animals, such as migratory habits. Freud plainly did not think of a *Trieb* as the same sort of thing. *Trieb* names something that is less reflexive and less specific than an instinct; it's more like an impulse, which was the translation

Bettelheim suggested. Drives can be (and, of course, generally are) displaced, redirected, and repressed—things it does not make sense to say about instincts.

Freud invented the death-drive in order to correct one of the flaws in his first system. That the term also functioned as a rebuke to the heterodoxy of two former disciples, Alfred Adler and Carl Jung, was probably not inadvertent. Originally, Freud had identified two types of drives: sexual drives (what Strachey termed "libido," though the German is blunter: *Lust*) and ego drives. (The German term that Strachey rendered as "ego" is simply *das Ich*—"the I.") These represent what Freud called the pleasure principle and the reality principle, and the crucial thing about these principles is that they are always in conflict. Conflict was important to Freud; conflict is where neurosis gets generated. The flaw emerged when Freud undertook, in 1914, to analyze narcissism—a sexual drive in the service of the ego. In principle, the libido can latch on to, or cathect with, any-thing. ("Cathexis" is another Stracheyism; Freud used an ordi-nary German word, *Besetzung*, which he thought could be translated as "interest.") This is why some people grow inordi-nately fond of other people's shoes. But to have the libido cathect with the self threatened to corrupt the absolute separa-tion between ego drives and sexual drives that Freud's system mandated. It came dangerously close to saying that the libido was behind everything, which happened to be the Jungian heresy. Freud might have replaced the ego drives with the con-cept of an aggressive impulse, but the concept of an aggressive impulse happened to be the Adlerian heresy, and Freud had already denounced it. In any case, a separate drive for aggression left the problem of sadism, an aggressive impulse that is also sexual.

Freud's solution was, characteristically, clever, counterintuitive, and beyond disproof. He set it out in *Beyond the Pleasure Principle*, where he redefined the drives. The new drives were the life-drive, which Freud called Eros, and the death-drive (which he did not call Thanatos; that name was introduced into the psychoanalytic literature by Freud's secretary, the analyst Paul Federn). Eros extended the scope of the sexual drive to include all the efforts that human beings make to, as Freud put it, "combine organic substances into ever larger unities"— to produce offspring, create communities, build cultures. Eros can operate, however, only by repressing a conflicting impulse, and this is the death-drive. Freud claimed a scientific basis for the death-drive: he offered biological evidence that all organic impulses are essentially conservative, and that one of those impulses is the impulse of the organism to return to an inorganic state. Why, then, does every creature appear to fend off threats to its survival instinctively? Because, Freud concluded, "the organism wishes to die only in its own fashion." This is why the death-impulse is not an instinct. It can be redirected outward, sparing the self, and take the form of aggression against others. "It is then," Freud said, "called the instinct of destruction, of mastery, the will to power." Sadism is therefore a redirection of a more primary impulse, masochism. We hurt others instead of ourselves because we wish to live a little longer, so that we may die on our own terms.

At first, Freud pretended to regard the concept of a death-drive as speculative and provisional—"until one has something better," as he explained to his analytic colleague and future biographer Ernest Jones. In fact, Freud was thrilled with his new idea. It seemed to him to make sense not only of sadism, masochism, aggression, and other destructive behaviors; it solved many other puzzles, as well. It explained the repetition compulsion associated with trauma—as in the case of the victims of shell shock, in the First World War, who could not stop reliving events that they had every reason to wish to forget. It even explained the tendency of analysis to fail, due to resistance and negative transference (hostility toward the analyst) on the part of the patient. As Freud concluded in one of his last essays, a piece with the monitory title "Analysis Terminable and Interminable," there must be something within the analysand that makes him or her prefer to suffer rather than change, and this something he associated with the death-drive. And opened out onto the realm of culture, Freud's new theory became the thesis of *Civilization and Its Discontents.* Culture is the by-product of the struggle between two "Heavenly powers," Eros and death. Eros makes us strive for harmony and unity; the *Todestrieb* explains why we will never get there. Once again, the individual parts map perfectly onto the social whole.

Freud was defensive about the death-drive because it was virtually the only one of his many "discoveries" for which his fellow analysts seemed to have no use. "The most bizarre monster of all his gallery of monsters," was the judgment of the English analyst William McDougall, in 1934. The therapeutic value of the concept is not obvious: it's hard to imagine an analyst explaining to a patient, "That's your death-drive acting up." Jones rejected the idea emphatically. Melanie Klein was nearly alone among prominent analysts in appropriating the term, and she used it to mean aggression, which is only part of what Freud intended. In the realm of cultural theory, though, the concept enjoyed a more interesting fate.

Of the many disciples to whose ambitions Freud gave shrewd and critical attention, Wilhelm Reich was far from the most significant. But there were two paths that Freud did not want psychoanalysis to go down. One was free love and the other was revolution, and Reich was trouble on both counts. He was an Austrian physician who became involved with the Vienna Psychoanalytic Polyclinic in the early 1920s. In 1927, he published *The Function of the Orgasm*, a book which argued that psychic health depends on orgasmic potency, which endorsed the principle of full sexual gratification, and which was dedicated to Freud. (Reich asked Freud to analyze him, but Freud declined.) In 1928, Reich joined the Communist Party, and, a year later, he toured the Soviet Union, where he advised audiences that Communism must be accompanied by sexual revolution if it hoped to survive. (He published his views, on his return, in a book called *The Sexual Revolution*.) It has been suggested that Reich's Russian lectures were the reason the Soviets banned psychoanalysis; whatever the truth, by 1930 Stalin had closed down the Russian Psychoanalytic Society (once a thriving organization) and Pavlovian behaviorism became the official psychology of the workers' state.

Soviet Communism is one of the few contemporary references Freud made in *Civilization and Its Discontents*. It was his example of a utopian, Eros-inspired project doomed to failure by the inexorability of the death-drive. "I have no concern with any economic criticisms of the communist system," Freud explained; "I cannot inquire into whether the abolition of private property is expedient or advantageous. But I am able to recognize that the psychological premises on which the system is based are an untenable illusion. . . . Aggressiveness was not created by property." Even if we were to abolish property, he argued, there would still be sexual jealousy. And (he was now plainly thinking of Reich) even "if we were to remove this factor, too, by allowing complete freedom of sexual life . . . we cannot, it is true, easily foresee what new paths the development of civilization could take; but one thing we can expect, and that is that this indestructible feature of human nature will follow it there." The death-instinct is biological, a feature of the organism. Civilization did not create it and civilization cannot, in the end, mitigate its demands. A few years after *Civilization and Its Discontents* appeared, Reich published an article on masochism in the *International Journal of Psychoanalysis*, an organ controlled by Freud. Freud permitted the article to be printed but he dissociated himself from what he called its "non-sensical statement that what we have called the death-instinct is a product of the capitalist system."

Hitler and Stalin destroyed psychoanalysis in Europe. It was, of course, a "Jewish science," and its practitioners—the ones who were not murdered—were forced to emigrate to England and the United States, a country which Freud (with no indication of ambivalence) held in contempt. The capital of the psychoanalytic movement was relocated from Vienna to New York City, where psychoanalysis developed in ways responsive to specifically American conditions of prosperity and conformity. Reich joined the exodus. He came to the United States in 1939 and enjoyed a vogue after the war as the inventor of the orgone energy accumulator—a specially designed box in which the patient sits and absorbs potency-enhancing cosmic rays. (Dwight Macdonald had one; so did Saul Bellow.) The Food and Drug Administration took a skeptical view of Reich's medical claims; Reich went to prison and died there, in 1957. It is easy to dismiss Reich as a deluded monomaniac (he was certainly a monomaniac), but he stands in a line of thought that is at the center of cold war intellectual debate. The debate was over the effort to tie psychic well-being to social change by bringing Freud together with Marx.

The central obstacle to this effort, as Freud himself had made quite clear, is the death-drive. If you accept Freudianism, you accept the *Todestrieb*, and if you want to perfect the race, or just make people happier, you have to deal with that "indestructible feature" of mental anatomy. Freud's hint, in *Civilization and Its Discontents*, that his new system implied a judgment on the utopian claims of Communism was not lost on cold war intellectuals. Lionel Trilling began his career at Columbia in the 1920s teaching, with his friend Jacques Barzun, a course called the Colloquium on Important Books—the prototype of the required undergraduate course at Columbia now called Contemporary Civilization. In the beginning, the final book Trilling and Barzun assigned was William James's *Principles of Psychology* (1890). (James was a favorite writer of Barzun's.) But after *Civilization and Its Discontents* appeared, Freud's book replaced James's at the end of the syllabus. For Trilling, who had been a Marxist and, briefly, a fellow traveler, Freud was the road *away* from Marx. Freud underwrote Trilling's anti-Communism.

The key to Trilling's thought—the reason he is such a complicated figure—was the notion that American liberalism shares a sacred principle of faith with Marxism, and even with Stalinism. This is the belief that individuals are products of their environments, and that people can therefore be made better, happier, worthier by changing the conditions in which they live. It is arguable whether the New Deal liberals of Trilling's time held to quite the same conception of historical materialism as Marx and Stalin, but Trilling was not interested in liberal politics (he was by no means a neoconservative himself); he was interested in liberal culture, in the kind of mentality that maintains a progressive, optimistic, therapeutic view of life, the mentality he satirized in the characters of Nancy and Arthur Croom in his novel, *The Middle of the Journey*, which was published in 1947. Trilling's most influential book, *The Liberal Imagination*, published three years later, was devoted to correcting this blindness in liberal culture.

Trilling took the death-drive in a literary sense. He was in no position to judge whether it stood up "under scientific inquiry," as he explained in a short book, published in 1955, called *Freud and the Crisis of Our Culture*. He understood it simply to name the element in the self that is permanently intractable to social conditioning. To this extent, he was following Freud. But Trilling had a twist. As a psychiatric method, psychoanalysis treats repression as a problem, the source of neuroses; in Trilling's view, Freudian theory showed that repression is not only necessary but good, and good not for the creation of culture but, precisely, for the building of character. In 1954, a psychiatric conference was held on the subject of loyalty oaths; the conferees concluded that loyalty oaths constituted a form of repression and were bound to have a bad effect on the nation's psychic health. Trilling took exception to this conclusion. Individuals are not so easily altered by social pressures, he insisted. Freud himself had lived in an official culture of anti-Semitism and, Trilling wrote, this "did not, so far as I can make out, impair the functioning of his ego or his super-ego." Liberal culture—a permissive, tolerant, people-helping culture—is bound, at a certain point, to hit an irrational resistance, much like the analyst does with the patient who fights improvement. Freud had argued that this resistance is the source of the individual's "discontents." (The German word is *Unbehagen*, which Freud thought could be translated as "discomfort." His first title for the book was *Das Unglück in der Kultur*, "Unhappiness in Culture.") Trilling thought, on the contrary, that the resistance of the death-drive was "liberating." For it operated as a kind of firewall against cultural control. Trilling converted the death-drive into the principle of nonconformity. His next two collections both took their titles from this idea. *The Opposing Self* and *Beyond Culture*.

Trilling's Freud was an answer to the Freud of the American psychoanalytic establishment in the 1950s, for which a healthy and well-adjusted ego, freed from resistance and repression, was the goal of analysis. His attack on this liberal brand of Freudianism was echoed by Phillip Rieff, in *Freud: The Mind of the Moralist*, in 1959. Rieff too understood the political message of Freud's theory of culture. "Revolution," he warned, "could only repeat the prototypal rebellion against the father, and in every case, like it, be doomed to failure." Properly understood, the true mission of psychoanalysis was the protection of the individual from society. "Psychoanalysis defends the private man against the demands made by both culture and instinct," Rieff wrote. An American postwar culture obsessed with adjustment and contentment might be as dangerous to the future of individual autonomy as the culture of turn-of-the-century Austria or Stalin's Russia.

The word "liberating" stands out in the writing of a critic as anti-Utopian and as drawn to a tragic view of life as Trilling was, but it reflected a genuine aspect of his thought, and it explains why he was attracted to one of the most radical interpretations of Freud ever made. Norman O. Brown's *Life against Death* was published in 1959 by Wesleyan University Press. (Brown was a classics professor at Wesleyan.) Two former Columbia students, Norman Podhoretz and Jason Epstein, read it and, as Podhoretz later recalled, recognized it as "a great book by a major thinker." They helped to get it reprinted in paperback. Trilling made *Life against Death* a selection of the book club (then called the Mid-Century Book Club) that he ran with Barzun and W. H. Auden, and he wrote a review calling it "one of the most interesting and valuable works of our time."

Brown took the death-instinct head-on. The problem wasn't the validity of the concept, he argued; the problem was the modern taboo against death. Freedom from sexual repression—specifically, the repression of the polymorphous-perverse impulses of infants—would re-eroticize the body, relieve us of the death-drive and its aggressive side-effects, and lead to an acceptance of death "as part of life." Trilling's fascination with this argument ended when, the following year, he invited Brown to Columbia to address the Phi Beta Kappa Society and listened to him praise the "supernatural powers" of madness. "Almost though not quite cant," Trilling called the speech in one of his last works, *Sincerity and Authenticity*, published in 1972 (a short work of intellectual history that might be described as the plot summary of the Colloquium on Important Books). In his final chapter, Trilling again called on Freud as a witness against utopias: *Civilization and Its Discontents*, he said, "may be thought to stand like a lion in the path of all hopes of achieving happiness through the radical revision of social life."

Life against Death enjoyed an enthusiastic reception as a Vintage paperback in the 1960s; it seemed to underwrite the liberationist attitude that was part of the spirit of the time. It was often linked with a work that Brown himself acknowledged with admiration, Herbert Marcuse's *Eros and Civilization*, which came out in 1955, four years before Brown's. Marcuse's book was a product of the long-term effort to devise an antitotalitarian Marxism undertaken by the thinkers associated with the Frankfurt School, whose members had emigrated in the same wave that brought so many European analysts to the United States. How Freud might figure in such a philosophy, and how psychoanalysis might explain contemporary events, such as the rise of totalitarianism and the Holocaust, was a matter of debate within the School. Marcuse engaged in a running dispute on these matters with the émigré psychologist Erich Fromm, who, in 1941, in a book that was influential in the United States, *Escape from Freedom*, analyzed the mass appeal of totalitarianism in Freudian terms. Two years later, in an article called "Individual and Mass Behavior," Bettelheim proposed a psychoanalytic explanation for what he reported as the tendency of inmates in concentration camps to identify with the guards. (Bettelheim's claims about prisoners in the camps were later disputed, but the article was widely read.) Fromm took pains, in *Escape from Freedom* and in a later book called *Anatomy of Human Destructiveness*, to discredit Freud's notion of the death-drive. Bettelheim, though, found it useful. "Without the concept of the death-drive," he later wrote, "some events of recent history—German history in particular—are incomprehensible."

In order to bring Freud into a Marxian critique, it was necessary to make the very move that Freud had taken pains not to authorize, which was to tie the neuroses to social conditions. Marxism is nothing if not historicist. Marcuse knew perfectly well, of course, that Freud's title referred to *Kultur;* but he chose to echo, in his own title, the English translation instead, apparently because although culture is with us willy-nilly—human beings produce culture in the same sense that they produce carbon-monoxide: they can't help it—civilizations are things that can be made, unmade, remade. They are historical phenomena. In the view of the leader of the Frankfurt School, Max Horkheimer, for example, the death-drive was a product not of biology, but of capitalism. He and Theodor Adorno invoked it to explain resistance to socialist reform, following Freud's use of it to explain resistance to treatment.

Marcuse's view was close to Reich's: if you got rid of capitalism and the patriarchal family, you could get rid of the oedipal complex and the oppressive super-ego it produced. Marcuse thought that the arrival of the postwar society of abundance might make obsolete Freud's notion of civilization as something whose survival requires self-punishing repression. For Marcuse, the goal of a Freudian revolution would be to release adults from the tyranny of genital sexuality, to return to the polymorphous perversity of childhood, and, by re-eroticizing man's relation to his own body and to nature, to overcome alienation. This would relax the grip of the super-ego and allow Eros to triumph. (Trilling was more comfortable with Marcuse's thesis than with Brown's because Marcuse held the counterculture and its "anything goes" rhetoric in contempt "repressive desublimation" was his term for it. Still, Trilling could not sign on to the program of polymorphous-perversity. "The development of genital sexuality is an arduous process which fulfills itself only through the renunciation of earlier modes of sexual gratification," he observed in *Sincerity and Authenticity*.)

The role played by revisionist Freudianism in social movements in the United States was relatively minor. Matters were different in France, where the brief insurrection of May 1968 was staged, quite self-consciously, as an attempt to free the psyche from the prison of consumerist heaven. One figure in that moment was the man who had become, after the wartime exodus, the most influential analyst in Europe, Jacques Lacan. Lacan joined the Société Psychanalytique de Paris in 1934; he was also close to, and influenced by, the group in France most receptive to Freudianism in Freud's lifetime, the surrealists. (Lacan sent his doctoral dissertation, on paranoia, to Freud, but they never met.) Lacan's theory, which he introduced in 1936 at a psychoanalytic congress in Marienbad, was based on the notion that the ego is an unreliable construction, whose "health" is, in fact, bad for the self. The ego emerges when the infant, at around a year old, identifies with other people or with its own image in the mirror. (This is what Lacan called the "mirror phase.") The ego that gets constructed from these identifications is alienated from the unconscious; this means that we cannot consciously know the difference between our desires and the desires of others. In Freudian terms, the ego controls and distorts the drives, and the purpose of analysis is to break through its obstructions. (Jones, who chaired the Marienbad conference, cut Lacan off after a few minutes of his paper—a brutal defense of orthodoxy but possibly suitable in the case of Lacan, who later became notorious for the "short session," in which analysis is terminated at some arbitrary point short of the canonical fifty minutes.)

Lacan was no biologist. He wasn't interested in understanding the mind anatomically; he understood it linguistically. He believed that the mind is made of meanings, learned from culture, and that the only way to get access to the unconscious is by analyzing the patient's use of language. But Lacan did believe in the death-drive—"the culminating point of Freud's doctrine," he called it in 1953 in a widely read paper, "The Function and Field of Speech and Language in Psychoanalysis." He thought it pointed to "a crack, a profound perturbation in the regulation of life." In other words, irruptions of the death-drive expose the facticity of the ego; they disrupt our illusion of autonomous selfhood, as the surrealists disrupt our illusions of temporal and spatial coherence and rationality. Lacan devoted his career to attacking the shibboleth of postwar analysis, the healthy ego. In 1951, he began directing biweekly seminars, in Paris, in which he "reread" Freud; after his only book, *Écrits*, was published, in 1966, the seminars became an intellectual sensation. When the revolutionary moment arrived, it was easy for Lacan's followers to take the road down which Reich and Marcuse (both of them also widely read by French radicals) had already traveled, and to associate the ego with postwar culture's false face of harmony and prosperity. Much of the metaphysical graffiti for which the events of May are known—"Take your desires for reality," "A policeman dwells in each of our heads; he must be killed"—derived from the Lacanian revision of Freud. Then, suddenly, it was June, and the revolution was over. Lacanian theory, along with every other branch of radical thought, left the streets. They have not been back.

It was pure perversity that led Freud's cold war readers to appropriate *Civilization and Its Discontents* for political purposes, whether conservative or radical in intent. For the whole point of that book would seem to be that politics doesn't matter— that as long as there is culture, people will be unhappy. But Freud's terms proved too powerful and suggestive to resist. "I have not the courage to rise up before my fellow-men as a prophet," Freud wrote at the end of his book, "and I bow to their reproach that I can offer them no consolation: for at bottom, that is what they are all demanding—the wildest revolutionaries no less passionately than the most virtuous believers." Whether this was modesty or only the rhetoric of modesty, Freud's readers understood him in the way they wanted to understand him. It is the fate of all mythmakers to be revised.

CIVILIZATION AND ITS DISCONTENTS

I

 I T IS IMPOSSIBLE to escape the impression that people commonly use false standards of measurement—that they seek power, success and wealth for themselves and admire them in others, and that they underestimate what is of true value in life. And yet, in making any general judgement of this sort, we are in danger of forgetting how variegated the human world and its mental life are. There are a few men from whom their contemporaries do not withhold admiration, although their greatness rests on attributes and achievements which are completely foreign to the aims and ideals of the multitude. One might easily be inclined to suppose that it is after all only a minority which appreciates these great men, while the large majority cares nothing for them. But things are probably not as simple as that, thanks to the discrepancies between people's thoughts and their actions, and to the diversity of their wishful impulses.

One of these exceptional few calls himself my friend in his

letters to me. I had sent him my small book that treats religion as an illusion,[1] and he answered that he entirely agreed with my judgement upon religion, but that he was sorry I had not properly appreciated the true source of religious sentiments. This, he says, consists in a peculiar feeling, which he himself is never without, which he finds confirmed by many others, and which he may suppose is present in millions of people. It is a feeling which he would like to call a sensation of 'eternity', a feeling as of something limitless, unbounded—as it were, 'oceanic'. This feeling, he adds, is a purely subjective fact, not an article of faith; it brings with it no assurance of personal immortality, but it is the source of the religious energy which is seized upon by the various Churches and religious systems, directed by them into particular channels, and doubtless also exhausted by them. One may, he thinks, rightly call oneself religious on the ground of this oceanic feeling alone, even if one rejects every belief and every illusion.

The views expressed by the friend whom I so much honour, and who himself once praised the magic of illusion in a poem,[2] caused me no small difficulty. I cannot discover this 'oceanic' feeling in myself. It is not easy to deal scientifically with feelings. One can attempt to describe their physiological signs. Where this is not possible—and I am afraid that the oceanic

[1] [*The Future of an Illusion* (1927c)].

[2] [*Footnote added* 1931:] *Liluli* [1919].—Since the publication of his two books *La vie de Ramakrishna* [1929] and *La vie de Vivekananda* (1930), I need no longer hide the fact that the friend spoken of in the text is Romain Rolland.

feeling too will defy this kind of characterization—nothing remains but to fall back on the ideational content which is most readily associated with the feeling. If I have understood my friend rightly, he means the same thing by it as the consolation offered by an original and somewhat eccentric dramatist to his hero who is facing a self-inflicted death. 'We cannot fall out of this world.'[3] That is to say, it is a feeling of an indissoluble bond, of being one with the external world as a whole. I may remark that to me this seems something rather in the nature of an intellectual perception, which is not, it is true, without an accompanying feeling-tone, but only such as would be present with any other act of thought of equal range. From my own experience I could not convince myself of the primary nature of such a feeling. But this gives me no right to deny that it does in fact occur in other people. The only question is whether it is being correctly interpreted and whether it ought to be regarded as the *fons et origo* of the whole need for religion.

I have nothing to suggest which could have a decisive influence on the solution of this problem. The idea of men's receiving an intimation of their connection with the world around them through an immediate feeling which is from the outset directed to that purpose sounds so strange and fits in so badly with the fabric of our psychology that one is justified in attempting to discover a psycho-analytic—that is, a genetic—

[3] Christian Dietrich Grabbe [1801–36], *Hannibal*: 'Ja, aus der Welt werden wir nicht fallen. Wir sind einmal darin.' ['Indeed, we shall not fall out of this world. We are in it once and for all.']

explanation of such a feeling. The following line of thought suggests itself. Normally, there is nothing of which we are more certain than the feeling of our self, of our own ego. This ego appears to us as something autonomous and unitary, marked off distinctly from everything else. That such an appearance is deceptive, and that on the contrary the ego is continued inwards, without any sharp delimitation, into an unconscious mental entity which we designate as the id and for which it serves as a kind of facade—this was a discovery first made by psycho-analytic research, which should still have much more to tell us about the relation of the ego to the id. But towards the outside, at any rate, the ego seems to maintain clear and sharp lines of demarcation. There is only one state— admittedly an unusual state, but not one that can be stigma- tized as pathological—in which it does not do this. At the height of being in love the boundary between ego and object threatens to melt away. Against all the evidence of his senses, a man who is in love declares that 'I' and 'you' are one, and is prepared to behave as if it were a fact. What can be temporar- ily done away with by a physiological [i.e. normal] function must also, of course, be liable to be disturbed by pathological processes. Pathology has made us acquainted with a great number of states in which the boundary lines between the ego and the external world become uncertain or in which they are actually drawn incorrectly. There are cases in which parts of a person's own body, even portions of his own mental life—his perceptions, thoughts and feelings—, appear alien to him and as not belonging to his ego; there are other cases in which he ascribes to the external world things that clearly originate in his own ego and that ought to be acknowledged by it. Thus even the feeling of our own ego is subject to disturbances and the boundaries of the ego are not constant.

Further reflection tells us that the adult's ego-feeling cannot have been the same from the beginning. It must have gone through a process of development, which cannot, of course, be demonstrated but which admits of being constructed with a fair degree of probability.[4] An infant at the breast does not as yet distinguish his ego from the external world as the source of the sensations flowing in upon him. He gradually learns to do so, in response to various promptings. He must be very strongly impressed by the fact that some sources of excitation, which he will later recognize as his own bodily organs, can provide him with sensations at any moment, whereas other sources evade him from time to time—among them what he desires most of all, his mother's breast—and only reappear as a result of his screaming for help. In this way there is for the first time set over against the ego an 'object', in the form of something which exists 'outside' and which is only forced to appear by a special action. A further incentive to a disengagement of the ego from the general mass of sensations—that is, to the recognition of an 'outside', an external world—is provided by

---

[4] Cf. the many writings on the topic of ego-development and ego-feeling, dating from Ferenczi's paper on 'Stages in the Development of the Sense of Reality' (1913) to Federn's contributions of 1926, 1927 and later.

the frequent, manifold and unavoidable sensations of pain and unpleasure the removal and avoidance of which is enjoined by the pleasure principle, in the exercise of its unrestricted domination. A tendency arises to separate from the ego everything that can become a source of such unpleasure, to throw it outside and to create a pure pleasure-ego which is confronted by a strange and threatening 'outside'. The boundaries of this primitive pleasure-ego cannot escape rectification through experience. Some of the things that one is unwilling to give up, because they give pleasure, are nevertheless not ego but object; and some sufferings that one seeks to expel turn out to be inseparable from the ego in virtue of their internal origin. One comes to learn a procedure by which, through a deliberate direction of one's sensory activities and through suitable muscular action, one can differentiate between what is internal—what belongs to the ego—and what is external—what emanates from the outer world. In this way one makes the first step towards the introduction of the reality principle which is to dominate future development. This differentiation, of course, serves the practical purpose of enabling one to defend oneself against sensations of unpleasure which one actually feels or with which one is threatened. In order to fend off certain unpleasurable excitations arising from within, the ego can use no other methods than those which it uses against unpleasure coming from without, and this is the starting-point of important pathological disturbances.

In this way, then, the ego detaches itself from the external world. Or, to put it more correctly, originally the ego includes everything, later it separates off an external world from itself. Our present ego-feeling is, therefore, only a shrunken residue of a much more inclusive—indeed, an all-embracing—feeling which corresponded to a more intimate bond between the ego and the world about it. If we may assume that there are many people in whose mental life this primary ego-feeling has persisted to a greater or less degree, it would exist in them side by side with the narrower and more sharply demarcated ego-feeling of maturity, like a kind of counterpart to it. In that case, the ideational contents appropriate to it would be precisely those of limitlessness and of a bond with the universe—the same ideas with which my friend elucidated the 'oceanic' feeling.

But have we a right to assume the survival of something that was originally there, alongside of what was later derived from it? Undoubtedly. There is nothing strange in such a phenomenon, whether in the mental field or elsewhere. In the animal kingdom we hold to the view that the most highly developed species have proceeded from the lowest; and yet we find all the simple forms still in existence to-day. The race of the great saurians is extinct and has made way for the mammals; but a true representative of it, the crocodile, still lives among us. This analogy may be too remote, and it is also weakened by the circumstance that the lower species which survive are for the most part not the true ancestors of the present-day more highly developed species. As a rule the intermediate links have died out and are known to us only through reconstruction. In the realm of the mind, on the other hand, what is primitive is so commonly preserved alongside of the transformed version which has arisen from it that it is unnecessary to give instances as evidence. When this happens it is usually in consequence of a divergence in development: one portion (in the quantitative sense) of an attitude or instinctual impulse has remained unaltered, while another portion has undergone further development.

This brings us to the more general problem of preservation in the sphere of the mind. The subject has hardly been studied as yet; but it is so attractive and important that we may be allowed to turn our attention to it for a little, even though our excuse is insufficient. Since we overcame the error of supposing that the forgetting we are familiar with signified a destruction of the memory-trace—that is, its annihilation—we have been inclined to take the opposite view, that in mental life nothing which has once been formed can perish—that everything is somehow preserved and that in suitable circumstances (when, for instance, regression goes back far enough) it can once more be brought to light. Let us try to grasp what this assumption involves by taking an analogy from another field. We will choose as an example the history of the Eternal City.[5] Historians tell us that the oldest Rome was the *Roma Quadrata*, a fenced settlement on the Palatine. Then followed the phase of the *Septimontium*, a federation of the settlements on the different hills; after that came the city bounded by the Servian wall;

[5] Based on *The Cambridge Ancient History*, 7 (1928): 'The Founding of Rome' by Hugh Last.

and later still, after all the transformations during the periods of the republic and the early Caesars, the city which the Emperor Aurelian surrounded with his walls. We will not follow the changes which the city went through any further, but we will ask ourselves how much a visitor, whom we will suppose to be equipped with the most complete historical and topographical knowledge, may still find left of these early stages in the Rome of to-day. Except for a few gaps, he will see the wall of Aurelian almost unchanged. In some places he will be able to find sections of the Servian wall where they have been excavated and brought to light. If he knows enough— more than present-day archaeology does—he may perhaps be able to trace out in the plan of the city the whole course of that wall and the outline of the *Roma Quadrata*. Of the buildings which once occupied this ancient area he will find nothing, or only scanty remains, for they exist no longer. The best information about Rome in the republican era would only enable him at the most to point out the sites where the temples and public buildings of that period stood. Their place is now taken by ruins, but not by ruins of themselves but of later restorations made after fires or destruction. It is hardly necessary to remark that all these remains of ancient Rome are found dovetailed into the jumble of a great metropolis which has grown up in the last few centuries since the Renaissance. There is certainly not a little that is ancient still buried in the soil of the city or beneath its modern buildings. This is the manner in which the past is preserved in historical sites like Rome.

Now let us, by a flight of imagination, suppose that Rome is not a human habitation but a psychical entity with a similarly long and copious past—an entity, that is to say, in which nothing that has once come into existence will have passed away and all the earlier phases of development continue to exist alongside the latest one. This would mean that in Rome the palaces of the Caesars and the Septizonium of Septimius Severus would still be rising to their old height on the Palatine and that the castle of S. Angelo would still be carrying on its battlements the beautiful statues which graced it until the siege by the Goths, and so on. But more than this. In the place occupied by the Palazzo Caffarelli would once more stand—without the Palazzo having to be removed—the Temple of Jupiter Capitolinus; and this not only in its latest shape, as the Romans of the Empire saw it, but also in its earliest one, when it still showed Etruscan forms and was ornamented with terra-cotta antefixes. Where the Coliseum now stands we could at the same time admire Nero's vanished Golden House. On the Piazza of the Pantheon we should find not only the Pantheon of today, as it was bequeathed to us by Hadrian, but, on the same site, the original edifice erected by Agrippa; indeed, the same piece of ground would be supporting the church of Santa Maria sopra Minerva and the ancient temple over which it was built. And the observer would perhaps only have to change the direction of his glance or his position in order to call up the one view or the other.

There is clearly no point in spinning our phantasy any further, for it leads to things that are unimaginable and even absurd. If we want to represent historical sequence in spatial terms we can only do it by juxtaposition in space: the same space cannot have two different contents. Our attempt seems to be an idle game. It has only one justification. It shows us how far we are from mastering the characteristics of mental life by representing them in pictorial terms.

There is one further objection which has to be considered. The question may be raised why we chose precisely the past of a *city* to compare with the past of the mind The assumption that everything past is preserved holds good even in mental life only on condition that the organ of the mind has remained intact and that its tissues have not been damaged by trauma or inflammation. But destructive influences which can be compared to causes of illness like these are never lacking in the history of a city, even if it has had a less chequered past than Rome, and even if, like London, it has hardly ever suffered from the visitations of an enemy. Demolitions and replacement of buildings occur in the course of the most peaceful development of a city. A city is thus *a priori* unsuited for a comparison of this sort with a mental organism.

We bow to this objection; and, abandoning our attempt to draw a striking contrast, we will turn instead to what is after all a more closely related object of comparison—the body of an animal or a human being. But here, too, we find the same thing. The earlier phases of development are in no sense still preserved; they have been absorbed into the later phases for which they have supplied the material. The embryo cannot be discovered in the adult. The thymus gland of childhood is replaced after puberty by connective tissue, but is no longer present itself; in the marrow-bones of the grown man I can, it is true, trace the outline of the child's bone, but it itself has disappeared, having lengthened and thickened until it has attained its definitive form. The fact remains that only in the mind is such a preservation of all the earlier stages alongside of the final form possible, and that we are not in a position to represent this phenomenon in pictorial terms.

Perhaps we are going too far in this. Perhaps we ought to content ourselves with asserting that what is past in mental life *may* be preserved and is not *necessarily* destroyed. It is always possible that even in the mind some of what is old is effaced or absorbed—whether in the normal course of things or as an exception—to such an extent that it cannot be restored or revivified by any means; or that preservation in general is dependent on certain favourable conditions. It is possible, but we know nothing about it. We can only hold fast to the fact that it is rather the rule than the exception for the past to be preserved in mental life.

Thus we are perfectly willing to acknowledge that the 'oceanic' feeling exists in many people, and we are inclined to trace it back to an early phase of ego-feeling. The further question then arises, what claim this feeling has to be regarded as the source of religious needs.

To me the claim does not seem compelling. After all, a feeling can only be a source of energy if it is itself the expression of a strong need. The derivation of religious needs from the infant's helplessness and the longing for the father aroused by it seems to me incontrovertible, especially since the feeling is not simply prolonged from childhood days, but is permanently sustained by fear of the superior power of Fate. I cannot think of any need in childhood as strong as the need for a father's protection. Thus the part played by the oceanic feeling, which might seek something like the restoration of limitless narcissism, is ousted from a place in the foreground. The origin of the religious attitude can be traced back in clear outlines as far as the feeling of infantile helplessness. There may be something further behind that, but for the present it is wrapped in obscurity.

I can imagine that the oceanic feeling became connected with religion later on. The 'oneness with the universe' which constitutes its ideational content sounds like a first attempt at a religious consolation, as though it were another way of disclaiming the danger which the ego recognizes as threatening it from the external world. Let me admit once more that it is very difficult for me to work with these almost intangible quantities. Another friend of mine, whose insatiable craving for knowledge has led him to make the most unusual experiments and has ended by giving him encyclopaedic knowledge, has assured me that through the practices of Yoga, by withdrawing from the world, by fixing the attention on bodily functions and by peculiar methods of breathing, one can in fact evoke new sensations and coenaesthesias in oneself, which he regards as regressions to primordial states of mind which have long ago been overlaid. He sees in them a physiological basis, as it were, of much of the wisdom of mysticism. It would not be hard to find connections here with a number of obscure modifications of mental life, such as trances and ecstasies. But I am moved to exclaim in the words of Schiller's diver:—

'. . . Es freue sich,
Wer da atmet im rosigten Licht,'[6]

---

[6] ['Let him rejoice who breathes up here in the roseate light!' Schiller, 'Der Taucher'.]

II

I N MY *Future of an Illusion* [1927c] I was concerned much less with the deepest sources of the religious feeling than with what the common man understands by his religion—with the system of doctrines and promises which on the one hand explains to him the riddles of this world with enviable completeness, and, on the other, assures him that a careful Providence will watch over his life and will compensate him in a future existence for any frustrations he suffers here. The common man cannot imagine this Providence otherwise than in the figure of an enormously exalted father. Only such a being can understand the needs of the children of men and be softened by their prayers and placated by the signs of their remorse. The whole thing is so patently infantile, so foreign to reality, that to anyone with a friendly attitude to humanity it is painful to think that the great majority of mortals will never be able to rise above this view of life. It is still more humiliating to discover how large a number of people living to-day, who cannot but see that this religion is not tenable, nevertheless try to defend it piece by piece in a series of pitiful rearguard actions. One would like to mix among the ranks of the believers in order to meet these philosophers, who think they can rescue the God of religion by replacing him by an impersonal, shadowy and abstract principle, and to address them with the warning words: 'Thou shalt not take the name of the Lord thy God in vain!' And if some of the great men of the past acted in the same way, no appeal can be made to their example: we know why they were obliged to.

Let us return to the common man and to his religion—the only religion which ought to bear that name. The first thing that we think of is the well-known saying of one of our great poets and thinkers concerning the relation of religion to art and science:

> *Wer Wissenschaft und Kunst besitzt, hat auch Religion;*
> *Wer jene beide nicht besitzt, der habe Religion!*[1]

This saying on the one hand draws an antithesis between religion and the two highest achievements of man, and on the other, asserts that, as regards their value in life, those achievements and religion can represent or replace each other. If we

---

[1] ['He who possesses science and art also has religion; but he who possesses neither of those two, let him have religion!']—Goethe, *Zahme Xenien* IX (Gedichte aus dem Nachlass).

also set out to deprive the common man, [who has neither science nor art] of his religion, we shall clearly not have the poet's
authority on our side. We will choose a particular path to bring
us nearer an appreciation of his words. Life, as we find it, is too
hard for us; it brings us too many pains, disappointments and
impossible tasks. In order to bear it we cannot dispense with
palliative measures. 'We cannot do without auxiliary construc-
tions', as Theodor Fontane tells us.[2] There are perhaps three
such measures: powerful deflections, which cause us to make
light of our misery; substitutive satisfactions, which diminish it;
and intoxicating substances, which make us insensitive to it.
Something of the kind is indispensable.[3] Voltaire has deflections in mind when he ends *Candide* with the advice to cultivate
one's garden; and scientific activity is a deflection of this kind,
too. The substitutive satisfactions, as offered by art, are illusions in contrast with reality, but they are none the less psychi-
cally effective, thanks to the role which phantasy has assumed
in mental life. The intoxicating substances influence our body
and alter its chemistry. It is no simple matter to see where religion has its place in this series. We must look further afield.

The question of the purpose of human life has been raised
countless times; it has never yet received a satisfactory answer
and perhaps does not admit of one. Some of those who have
asked it have added that if it should turn out that life has *no*

[2] [It has not been possible to trace this quotation.]
[3] In *Die Fromme Helene* Wilhelm Busch has said the same thing on a lower plane:
'Wer Sorgen hat, hat auch Likör.' ['He who has cares has brandy too.']

purpose, it would lose all value for them. But this threat alters nothing. It looks, on the contrary, as though one had a right to dismiss the question, for it seems to derive from the human presumptuousness, many other manifestations of which are already familiar to us. Nobody talks about the purpose of the life of animals, unless, perhaps, it may be supposed to lie in being of service to man. But this view is not tenable either, for there are many animals of which man can make nothing, except to describe, classify and study them; and innumerable species of animals have escaped even this use, since they existed and became extinct before man set eyes on them. Once again, only religion can answer the question of the purpose of life. One can hardly be wrong in concluding that the idea of life having a purpose stands and falls with the religious system.

We will therefore turn to the less ambitious question of what men themselves show by their behaviour to be the purpose and intention of their lives. What do they demand of life and wish to achieve in it? The answer to this can hardly be in doubt. They strive after happiness; they want to become happy and to remain so. This endeavour has two sides, a positive and a negative aim. It aims, on the one hand, at an absence of pain and unpleasure, and, on the other, at the experiencing of strong feelings of pleasure. In its narrower sense the word 'happiness' only relates to the last. In conformity with this dichotomy in his aims, man's activity develops in two directions, according as it seeks to realize—in the main, or even exclusively—the one or the other of these aims.

As we see, what decides the purpose of life is simply the programme of the pleasure principle. This principle dominates the
operation of the mental apparatus from the start. There can be
no doubt about its efficacy, and yet its programme is at logger-
heads with the whole world, with the macrocosm as much as
with the microcosm. There is no possibility at all of its being
carried through; all the regulations of the universe run counter
to it. One feels inclined to say that the intention that man
should be 'happy' is not included in the plan of 'Creation'.
What we call happiness in the strictest sense comes from the
(preferably sudden) satisfaction of needs which have been
dammed up to a high degree, and it is from its nature only possible as an episodic phenomenon. When any situation that is
desired by the pleasure principle is prolonged, it only produces
a feeling of mild contentment. We are so made that we can
derive intense enjoyment only from a contrast and very little
from a state of things.[4] Thus our possibilities of happiness are
already restricted by our constitution. Unhappiness is much
less difficult to experience. We are threatened with suffering
from three directions: from our own body, which is doomed to
decay and dissolution and which cannot even do without pain

---

[4] Goethe, indeed, warns us that 'nothing is harder to bear than a succession of
fair days.'

> [Alles in der Welt lässt sich ertragen,
> Nur nicht eine Reihe von schönen
> Tagen.
> (Weimar, 1810–12.)]

But this may be an exaggeration.

and anxiety as warning signals; from the external world, which may rage against us with overwhelming and merciless forces of destruction; and finally from our relations to other men. The suffering which comes from this last source is perhaps more painful to us than any other. We tend to regard it as a kind of gratuitous addition, although it cannot be any less fatefully inevitable than the suffering which comes from elsewhere.

It is no wonder if, under the pressure of these possibilities of suffering, men are accustomed to moderate their claims to happiness—just as the pleasure principle itself, indeed, under the influence of the external world, changed into the more modest reality principle—, if a man thinks himself happy merely to have escaped unhappiness or to have survived his suffering, and if in general the task of avoiding suffering pushes that of obtaining pleasure into the background. Reflection shows that the accomplishment of this task can be attempted along very different paths; and all these paths have been recommended by the various schools of worldly wisdom and put into practice by men. An unrestricted satisfaction of every need presents itself as the most enticing method of conducting one's life, but it means putting enjoyment before caution, and soon brings its own punishment. The other methods, in which avoidance of unpleasure is the main purpose, are differentiated according to the source of unpleasure to which their attention is chiefly turned. Some of these methods are extreme and some moderate; some are one-sided and some attack the problem simultaneously at several points. Against the suffering which may come upon one from human relationships the readiest safeguard is voluntary isolation, keeping oneself aloof from other people. The happiness which can be achieved along this path is, as we see, the happiness of quietness. Against the dreaded external world one can only defend oneself by some kind of turning away from it, if one intends to solve the task by oneself. There is, indeed, another and better path: that of becoming a member of the human community, and, with the help of a technique guided by science, going over to the attack against nature and subjecting her to the human will. Then one is working with all for the good of all. But the most interesting methods of averting suffering are those which seek to influence our own organism. In the last analysis, all suffering is nothing else than sensation; it only exists in so far as we feel it, and we only feel it in consequence of certain ways in which our organism is regulated.

The crudest, but also the most effective among these methods of influence is the chemical one—intoxication. I do not think that anyone completely understands its mechanism, but it is a fact that there are foreign substances which, when present in the blood or tissues, directly cause us pleasurable sensations; and they also so alter the conditions governing our sensibility that we become incapable of receiving unpleasurable impulses. The two effects not only occur simultaneously, but seem to be intimately bound up with each other. But there must be substances in the chemistry of our own bodies which have similar effects, for we know at least one pathological state, mania, in which a condition similar to intoxication arises without the administration of any intoxicating drug. Besides this, our normal mental life exhibits oscillations between a comparatively easy liberation of pleasure and a comparatively difficult one, parallel with which there goes a diminished or an increased receptivity to unpleasure. It is greatly to be regretted that this toxic side of mental processes has so far escaped scientific examination. The service rendered by intoxicating media in the struggle for happiness and in keeping misery at a distance is so highly prized as a benefit that individuals and peoples alike have given them an established place in the economics of their libido. We owe to such media not merely the immediate yield of pleasure, but also a greatly desired degree of independence from the external world. For one knows that, with the help of this 'drowner of cares' one can at any time withdraw from the pressure of reality and find refuge in a world of one's own with better conditions of sensibility. As is well known, it is precisely this property of intoxicants which also determines their danger and their injuriousness. They are responsible, in certain circumstances, for the useless waste of a large quota of energy which might have been employed for the improvement of the human lot.

The complicated structure of our mental apparatus admits, however, of a whole number of other influences. Just as a satisfaction of instinct spells happiness for us, so severe suffering is caused us if the external world lets us starve, if it refuses to sate our needs. One may therefore hope to be freed from a part of one's sufferings by influencing the instinctual impulses. This

CIVILIZATION AND ITS DISCONTENTS

type of defence against suffering is no longer brought to bear on the sensory apparatus; it seeks to master the internal sources of our needs. The extreme form of this is brought about by killing off the instincts, as is prescribed by the worldly wisdom of the East and practised by Yoga. If it succeeds, then the subject has, it is true, given up all other activities as well—he has sacrificed his life; and, by another path, he has once more only achieved the happiness of quietness. We follow the same path when our aims are less extreme and we merely attempt to *control* our instinctual life. In that case, the controlling elements are the higher psychical agencies, which have subjected themselves to the reality principle. Here the aim of satisfaction is not by any means relinquished; but a certain amount of protection against suffering is secured, in that non-satisfaction is not so painfully felt in the case of instincts kept in dependence as in the case of uninhibited ones. As against this, there is an undeniable diminution in the potentialities of enjoyment. The feeling of happiness derived from the satisfaction of a wild instinctual impulse untamed by the ego is incomparably more intense than that derived from sating an instinct that has been tamed. The irresistibility of perverse instincts, and perhaps the attraction in general of forbidden things finds an economic explanation here.

Another technique for fending off suffering is the employment of the displacements of libido which our mental apparatus permits of and through which its function gains so much in flexibility. The task here is that of shifting the instinctual aims in such a way that they cannot come up against frustration from the external world. In this, sublimation of the instincts lends its assistance. One gains the most if one can sufficiently heighten the yield of pleasure from the sources of psychical and intellectual work. When that is so, fate can do little against one. A satisfaction of this kind, such as an artist's joy in creating, in giving his phantasies body, or a scientist's in solving problems or discovering truths, has a special quality which we shall certainly one day be able to characterize in metapsychological terms. At present we can only say figuratively that such satisfactions seem 'finer and higher'. But their intensity is mild as compared with that derived from the sating of crude and primary instinctual impulses; it does not convulse our physical being. And the weak point of this method is that it is not applicable generally: it is accessible to only a few people. It presupposes the possession of special dispositions and gifts which are far from being common to any practical degree. And even to the few who do possess them, this method cannot give complete protection from suffering. It creates no impenetrable armour against the arrows of fortune, and it habitually fails when the source of suffering is a person's own body.[5]

[5] When there is no special disposition in a person which imperatively prescribes what direction his interest in life shall take, the ordinary professional work that is open to everyone can play the part assigned to it by Voltaire's wise advice [p. 51 above]. It is not possible, within the limits of a short survey, to discuss adequately the significance of work for the economics of the libido. No other technique for the conduct of life attaches the individual so firmly to reality as laying emphasis on work; for his work at least gives him a secure place in a portion of reality, in the human community. The possibility it offers of displacing a large amount of libidinal

While this procedure already clearly shows an intention of making oneself independent of the external world by seeking satisfaction in internal, psychical processes, the next procedure brings out those features yet more strongly. In it, the connection with reality is still further loosened; satisfaction is obtained from illusions, which are recognized as such without the discrepancy between them and reality being allowed to interfere with enjoyment. The region from which these illusions arise is the life of the imagination; at the time when the development of the sense of reality took place, this region was expressly exempted from the demands of reality-testing and was set apart for the purpose of fulfilling wishes which were difficult to carry out. At the head of these satisfactions through phantasy stands the enjoyment of works of art—an enjoyment which, by the agency of the artist, is made accessible even to those who are not themselves creative.[6] People who are receptive to the influence of art cannot set too high a value on it as

---

components, whether narcissistic, aggressive or even erotic, on to professional work and on to the human relations connected with it lends it a value by no means second to what it enjoys as something indispensible to the preservation and justification of existence in society. Professional activity is a source of special satisfaction if it is a freely chosen one—if, that is to say, by means of sublimation, it makes possible the use of existing inclinations, of persisting or constitutionally reinforced instinctual impulses. And yet, as a path to happiness, work is not highly prized by men. They do not strive after it as they do after other possibilities of satisfaction. The great majority of people only work under the stress of necessity, and this natural human aversion to work raises most difficult social problems.

[6] Cf. 'Formulations on the Two Principles of Mental Functioning' (1911b), and Lecture XXIII of my *Introductory Lectures* (1916–17).

a source of pleasure and consolation in life. Nevertheless the mild narcosis induced in us by art can do no more than bring about a transient withdrawal from the pressure of vital needs, and it is not strong enough to make us forget real misery.

Another procedure operates more energetically and more thoroughly. It regards reality as the sole enemy and as the source of all suffering, with which it is impossible to live, so that one must break off all relations with it if one is to be in any way happy. The hermit turns his back on the world and will have no truck with it. But one can do more than that; one can try to re-create the world, to build up in its stead another world in which its most unbearable features are eliminated and replaced by others that are in conformity with one's own wishes. But whoever, in desperate defiance, sets out upon this path to happiness will as a rule attain nothing. Reality is too strong for him. He becomes a madman, who for the most part finds no one to help him in carrying through his delusion. It is asserted, however, that each one of us behaves in some one respect like a paranoic, corrects some aspect of the world which is unbearable to him by the construction of a wish and intro-duces this delusion into reality. A special importance attaches to the case in which this attempt to procure a certainty of hap-piness and a protection against suffering through a delusional remoulding of reality is made by a considerable number of peo-ple in common. The religions of mankind must be classed among the mass-delusions of this kind. No one, needless to say, who shares a delusion ever recognizes it as such.

I do not think that I have made a complete enumeration of the methods by which men strive to gain happiness and keep suffering away and I know, too, that the material might have been differently arranged. One procedure I have not yet mentioned—not because I have forgotten it but because it will concern us later in another connection. And how could one possibly forget, of all others, this technique in the art of living? It is conspicuous for a most remarkable combination of characteristic features. It, too, aims of course at making the subject independent of Fate (as it is best to call it), and to that end it locates satisfaction in internal mental processes, making use, in so doing, of the displaceability of the libido of which we have already spoken [p. 56]. But it does not turn away from the external world, on the contrary, it clings to the objects belonging to that world and obtains happiness from an emotional relationship to them. Nor is it content to aim at an avoidance of unpleasure—a goal, as we might call it, of weary resignation; it passes this by without heed and holds fast to the original, passionate striving for a positive fulfilment of happiness. And perhaps it does in fact come nearer to this goal than any other method. I am, of course, speaking of the way of life which makes love the centre of everything, which looks for all satisfaction in loving and being loved. A psychical attitude of this sort comes naturally enough to all of us; one of the forms in which love manifests itself—sexual love—has given us our most intense experience of an overwhelming sensation of pleasure and has thus furnished us with a pattern for our search

for happiness. What is more natural than that we should per-
sist in looking for happiness along the path on which we first
encountered it? The weak side of this technique of living is
easy to see; otherwise no human being would have thought of
abandoning this path to happiness for any other. It is that we
are never so defenceless against suffering as when we love,
never so helplessly unhappy as when we have lost our loved
object or its love. But this does not dispose of the technique of
living based on the value of love as a means to happiness.
There is much more to be said about it. [See below, p. 88]

We may go on from here to consider the interesting case in
which happiness in life is predominantly sought in the enjoyment of beauty, wherever beauty presents itself to our senses
and our judgement—the beauty of human forms and gestures,
of natural objects and landscapes and of artistic and even scientific creations. This aesthetic attitude to the goal of life
offers little protection against the threat of suffering, but it can
compensate for a great deal. The enjoyment of beauty has a
peculiar, mildly intoxicating quality of feeling. Beauty has no
obvious use; nor is there any clear cultural necessity for it. Yet
civilization could not do without it. The science of aesthetics
investigates the conditions under which things are felt as beautiful, but it has been unable to give any explanation of the
nature and origin of beauty, and, as usually happens, lack of
success is concealed beneath a flood of resounding and empty
words. Psychoanalysis, unfortunately, has scarcely anything to
say about beauty either. All that seems certain is its derivation

from the field of sexual feeling. The love of beauty seems a perfect example of an impulse inhibited in its aim. 'Beauty' and 'attraction'[7] are originally attributes of the sexual object. It is worth remarking that the genitals themselves, the sight of which is always exciting, are nevertheless hardly ever judged to be beautiful; the quality of beauty seems, instead, to attach to certain secondary sexual characters.

In spite of the incompleteness [of my enumeration], I will venture on a few remarks as a conclusion to our enquiry. The programme of becoming happy, which the pleasure principle imposes on us, cannot be fulfilled; yet we must not—indeed, we cannot—give up our efforts to bring it nearer to fulfillment by some means or other. Very different paths may be taken in that direction, and we may give priority either to the positive aspect of the aim, that of gaining pleasure, or to its negative one, that of avoiding unpleasure. By none of these paths can we attain all that we desire. Happiness, in the reduced sense in which we recognize it as possible, is a problem of the economics of the individual's libido. There is no golden rule which applies to everyone: every man must find out for himself in what particular fashion he can be saved.[8] All kinds of different factors will operate to direct his choice. It is a question of how much real satisfaction he can expect to get from the external

[7] [The German 'Reiz' means 'stimulus' as well as 'charm' or 'attraction'.]

[8] [The allusion is to a saying attributed to Frederick the Great: 'in my State every man can be saved after his own fashion.' Freud had quoted this a short time before, in *Lay Analysis* (1926e), *Standard Ed.*, 20, 236.]

world, how far he is led to make himself independent of it, and, finally, how much strength he feels he has for altering the world to suit his wishes. In this, his psychical constitution will play a decisive part, irrespectively of the external circumstances. The man who is predominantly erotic will give first preference to his emotional relationships to other people; the narcissistic man, who inclines to be self-sufficient, will seek his main satisfactions in his internal mental processes; the man of action will never give up the external world on which he can try out his strength. As regards the second of these types, the nature of his talents and the amount of instinctual sublimation open to him will decide where he shall locate his interests. Any choice that is pushed to an extreme will be penalized by exposing the individual to the dangers which arise if a technique of living that has been chosen as an exclusive one should prove inadequate. Just as a cautious business-man avoids tying up all his capital in one concern, so, perhaps, worldly wisdom will advise us not to look for the whole of our satisfaction from a single aspiration. Its success is never certain, for that depends on the convergence of many factors, perhaps on none more than on the capacity of the psychical constitution to adapt its function to the environment and then to exploit that environment for a yield of pleasure. A person who is born with a specially unfavourable instinctual constitution, and who has not properly undergone the transformation and rearrangement of his libidinal components which is indispensable for later achievements, will find it hard to obtain happiness from his external situation, especially if he is faced with tasks of some difficulty. As a last technique of living, which will at least bring him substitutive satisfactions, he is offered that of a flight into neurotic illness—a flight which he usually accomplishes when he is still young. The man who sees his pursuit of happiness come to nothing in later years can still find consolation in the yield of pleasure of chronic intoxication, or he can embark on the desperate attempt at rebellion seen in a psychosis.[9]

Religion restricts this play of choice and adaptation, since it imposes equally on everyone its own path to the acquisition of happiness and protection from suffering. Its technique consists in depressing the value of life and distorting the picture of the real world in a delusional manner—which presupposes an intimidation of the intelligence. At this price, by forcibly fixing them in a state of psychical infantilism and by drawing them into a mass-delusion, religion succeeds in sparing many people an individual neurosis. But hardly anything more. There are, as we have said, many paths which *may* lead to such happiness as is attainable by men, but there is none which does so for certain. Even religion cannot keep its promise. If the

---

[9] [*Footnote added* 1931:] I feel impelled to point out one at least of the gaps that have been left in the account given above. No discussion of the possibilities of human happiness should omit to take into consideration the relation between narcissism and object libido. We require to know what being essentially self-dependent signifies for the economics of the libido.

believer finally sees himself obliged to speak of God's 'inscrutable decrees', he is admitting that all that is left to him as a last possible consolation and source of pleasure in his suffering is an unconditional submission. And if he is prepared for that, he could probably have spared himself the *détour* he has made.

III

Our enquiry concerning happiness has not so far taught us much that is not already common knowledge. And even if we proceed from it to the problem of why it is so hard for men to be happy, there seems no greater prospect of learning anything new. We have given the answer already by pointing to the three sources from which our suffering comes: the superior power of nature, the feebleness of our own bodies and the inadequacy of the regulations which adjust the mutual relationships of human beings in the family, the state and society. In regard to the first two sources, our judgement cannot hesitate long. It forces us to acknowledge those sources of suffering and to submit to the inevitable. We shall never completely master nature; and our bodily organism, itself a part of that nature, will always remain a transient structure with a limited capacity for adaptation and achievement. This recognition does not have a paralysing effect. On the contrary, it points the direction for our activity. If we cannot remove all suffering, we can remove some, and we can mitigate some: the experience of many thousands of years has convinced us of that. As regards the third source, the social source of suffering, our attitude is a different one. We do not admit it at all; we cannot see why the regulations made by ourselves should not, on the contrary, be a protection and a benefit for every one of us. And yet, when we consider how unsuccessful we have been in precisely this field of prevention of suffering, a suspicion dawns on us that here, too, a piece of unconquerable nature may lie behind—this time a piece of our own psychical constitution.

When we start considering this possibility, we come upon a contention which is so astonishing that we must dwell upon it. This contention holds that what we call our civilization is largely responsible for our misery, and that we should be much happier if we gave it up and returned to primitive conditions. I call this contention astonishing because, in whatever way we may define the concept of civilization, it is a certain fact that all the things with which we seek to protect ourselves against the threats that emanate from the sources of suffering are part of that very civilization.

How has it happened that so many people have come to take up this strange attitude of hostility to civilization? I believe that the basis of it was a deep and long-standing dissatisfaction with the then existing state of civilization and that on that basis a condemnation of it was built up, occasioned by certain specific historical events. I think I know what the last and the last but one of those occasions were. I am not learned enough to trace the chain of them far back enough in the history of the human species; but a factor of this kind hostile to civilization must already have been at work in the victory of Christendom over the heathen religions. For it was very closely related to the low estimation put upon earthly life by the Christian doctrine. The last but one of these occasions was when the progress of voyages of discovery led to contact with primitive peoples and races. In consequence of insufficient observation and a mistaken view of their manners and customs, they appeared to Europeans to be leading a simple, happy life with few wants, a life such as was unattainable by their visitors with their superior civilization. Later experience has corrected some of those judgements. In many cases the observers had wrongly attributed to the absence of complicated cultural demands what was in fact due to the bounty of nature and the ease with which the major human needs were satisfied. The last occasion is especially familiar to us. It arose when people came to know about the mechanism of the neuroses, which threaten to undermine the modicum of happiness enjoyed by civilized men. It was discovered that a person becomes neurotic because he cannot tolerate the amount of frustration which society imposes on him in the service of its cultural ideals, and it was inferred from this that the abolition or reduction of those demands would result in a return to possibilities of happiness.

There is also an added factor of disappointment. During the last few generations mankind has made an extraordinary advance in the natural sciences and in their technical application and has established his control over nature in a way never before imagined. The single steps of this advance are common knowledge and it is unnecessary to enumerate them. Men are proud of those achievements, and have a right to be. But they seem to have observed that this newly-won power over space and time, this subjugation of the forces of nature, which is the fulfillment of a longing that goes back thousands of years, has not increased the amount of pleasurable satisfaction which they may expect from life and has not made them feel happier. From the recognition of this fact we ought to be content to conclude that power over nature is not the *only* precondition of human happiness, just as it is not the *only* goal of cultural endeavour; we ought not to infer from it that technical progress is without value for the economics of our happiness. One would like to ask: is there, then, no positive gain in pleasure, no unequivocal increase in my feeling of happiness, if I can, as often as I please, hear the voice of a child of mine who is living hundreds of miles away or if I can learn in the shortest possible time after a friend has reached his destination that he has come through the long and difficult voyage unharmed? Does it mean nothing that medicine has succeeded in enormously reducing infant mortality and the danger of infection for women in childbirth, and, indeed, in considerably lengthening the average life of a civilized man? And there is a long list that might be added to benefits of this kind which we owe to the much-despised era of scientific and technical advances.

But here the voice of pessimistic criticism makes itself heard and warns us that most of these satisfactions follow the model of the 'cheap enjoyment' extolled in the anecdote—the enjoyment obtained by putting a bare leg from under the bedclothes on a cold winter night and drawing it in again. If there had been no railway to conquer distances, my child would never have left his native town and I should need no telephone to hear his voice; if travelling across the ocean by ship had not been introduced, my friend would not have embarked on his sea-voyage and I should not need a cable to relieve my anxiety about him. What is the use of reducing infantile mortality when it is precisely that reduction which imposes the greatest restraint on us in the begetting of children, so that, taken all round, we nevertheless rear no more children than in the days before the reign of hygiene, while at the same time we have created difficult conditions for our sexual life in marriage, and have probably worked against the beneficial effects of natural selection? And, finally, what good to us is a long life if it is difficult and barren of joys and if it is so full of misery that we can only welcome death as a deliverer?

It seems certain that we do not feel comfortable in our present-day civilization, but it is very difficult to form an opinion whether and in what degree men of an earlier age felt happier and what part their cultural conditions played in the matter. We shall always tend to consider people's distress objectively—that is, to place ourselves, with our own wants and sensibilities, in their conditions, and then to examine what occasions we should find in them for experiencing happiness or unhappiness. This method of looking at things, which seems objective because it ignores the variations in subjective sensibility, is, of course, the most subjective possible, since it puts one's own mental states in the place of any others, unknown though they may be. Happiness, however, is something essentially subjective. No matter how much we may shrink with horror from certain situations—of a galley-slave in antiquity, of a peasant during the Thirty Years' War, of a victim of the Holy Inquisition, of a Jew awaiting a pogrom—it is nevertheless impossible for us to feel our way into such people—to divine the changes which original obtuseness of mind, a gradual stupefying process, the cessation of expectations, and cruder or more refined methods of narcotization have produced upon their receptivity to sensations of pleasure and unpleasure. Moreover, in the case of the most extreme possibility of suffering, special mental protective devices are brought into operation. It seems to me unprofitable to pursue this aspect of the problem any further.

It is time for us to turn our attention to the nature of this civilization on whose value as a means to happiness doubts have been thrown. We shall not look for a formula in which to express that nature in a few words, until we have learned something by examining it. We shall therefore content ourselves with saying once more that the word 'civilization'[1] describes

---

[1] 'Kultur.' For the translation of this word see the Editor's Note to *The Future of an Illusion*.

the whole sum of the achievements and the regulations which distinguish our lives from those of our animal ancestors and which serve two purposes—namely to protect men against nature and to adjust their mutual relations.[2] In order to learn more, we will bring together the various features of civilization individually, as they are exhibited in human communities. In doing so, we shall have no hesitation in letting ourselves be guided by linguistic usage or, as it is also called, linguistic feeling, in the conviction that we shall thus be doing justice to inner discernments which still defy expression in abstract terms.

The first stage is easy. We recognize as cultural all activities and resources which are useful to men for making the earth serviceable to them, for protecting them against the violence of the forces of nature, and so on. As regards this side of civilization, there can be scarcely any doubt. If we go back far enough, we find that the first acts of civilization were the use of tools, the gaining of control over fire and the construction of dwellings. Among these, the control over fire stands out as a quite extraordinary and unexampled achievement,[3] while the

---

[2] See *The Future of an Illusion.*

[3] Psycho-analytic material, incomplete as it is and not susceptible to clear interpretation, nevertheless admits of a conjecture—a fantastic-sounding one—about the origin of this human feat. It is as though primal man had the habit, when he came in contact with fire, of satisfying an infantile desire connected with it, by putting it out with a stream of his urine. The legends that we possess leave no doubt about the originally phallic view taken of tongues of flame as they shoot upwards. Putting out fire by micturating—a theme to which modern giants, Gulliver in Lilliput and Rabelais' Gargantua, still hark back—was therefore a kind of sexual act

others opened up paths which man has followed ever since, and the stimulus to which is easily guessed. With every tool man is perfecting his own organs, whether motor or sensory, or is removing the limits to their functioning. Motor power places gigantic forces at his disposal, which, like his muscles, he can employ in any direction; thanks to ships and aircraft neither water nor air can hinder his movements; by means of spectacles he corrects defects in the lens of his own eye; by means of the telescope he sees into the far distance; and by means of the microscope he overcomes the limits of visibility set by the structure of his retina. In the photographic camera he has created an instrument which retains the fleeting visual impressions, just as a gramophone disc retains the equally fleeting auditory ones; both are at bottom materializations of the power he possesses of recollection, his memory. With the help of the telephone he can hear at distances which would be respected as unattainable even in a fairy tale. Writing was in its

---

with a male, an enjoyment of sexual potency in a homosexual competition. The first person to renounce this desire and spare the fire was able to carry it off with him and subdue it to his own use. By damping down the fire of his own sexual excitation, he had tamed the natural force of fire. This great cultural conquest was thus the reward for his renunciation of instinct. Further, it is as though woman had been appointed guardian of the fire which was held captive on the domestic hearth, because her anatomy made it impossible for her to yield to the temptation of this desire. It is remarkable, too, how regularly analytic experience testifies to the connection between ambition, fire and urethral erotism.—[Freud had pointed to the connection between urination and fire as early as in the 'Dora' case history (1905e [1901]). The connection with ambition came rather later. A full list of references will be found in the Editor's Note to the later paper on the subject, 'The Acquisition and Control of Fire' (1932a).]

origin the voice of an absent person; and the dwelling-house was a substitute for the mother's womb, the first lodging, for which in all likelihood man still longs, and in which he was safe and felt at ease.

These things that, by his science and technology, man has brought about on this earth, on which he first appeared as a feeble animal organism and on which each individual of his species must once more make its entry ('oh inch of nature '4) as a helpless suckling—these things do not only sound like a fairy tale, they are an actual fulfilment of every—or of almost every—fairy-tale wish. All these assets he may lay claim to as his cultural acquisition. Long ago he formed an ideal conception of omnipotence and omniscience which he embodied in his gods. To these gods he attributed everything that seemed unattainable to his wishes, or that was forbidden to him. One may say, therefore, that these gods were cultural ideals. To-day he has come very close to the attainment of this ideal, he has almost become a god himself. Only, it is true, in the fashion in

---

4 [In English in the original. This very Shakespearean phrase is not in fact to be found in the canon of Shakespeare. The words 'Poore inch of Nature' occur, however, in a novel by George Wilkins, *The Painfull Adventures of Pericles Prince of Tyre*, where they are addressed by Pericles to his infant daughter. This work was first printed in 1608, just after the publication of Shakespeare's play, in which Wilkins has been thought to have had a hand. Freud's unexpected acquaintance with the phrase is explained by its appearance in a discussion of the origins of *Pericles* in Georg Brandes's well-known book on Shakespeare, a copy of the German translation of which had a place in Freud's library (Brandes, 1896). He is known to have greatly admired the Danish critic (cf. Jones, 1957, 120), and the same book is quoted in his paper on the three caskets (1913f).]

which ideals are usually attained according to the general judgement of humanity. Not completely; in some respects not at all, in others only half way. Man has, as it were, become a kind of prosthetic God. When he puts on all his auxiliary organs he is truly magnificent; but those organs have not grown on to him and they still give him much trouble at times. Nevertheless, he is entitled to console himself with the thought that this development will not come to an end precisely with the year 1930 A.D. Future ages will bring with them new and probably unimaginably great advances in this field of civilization and will increase man's likeness to God still more. But in the interests of our investigations, we will not forget that present-day man does not feel happy in his Godlike character.

We recognize, then, that countries have attained a high level of civilization if we find that in them everything which can assist in the exploitation of the earth by man and in his protection against the forces of nature—everything, in short, which is of use to him—is attended to and effectively carried out. In such countries rivers which threaten to flood the land are regulated in their flow, and their water is directed through canals to places where there is a shortage of it. The soil is carefully cultivated and planted with the vegetation which it is suited to support; and the mineral wealth below ground is assiduously brought to the surface and fashioned into the required implements and utensils. The means of communication are ample, rapid and reliable. Wild and dangerous animals have been exterminated, and the breeding of domesticated animals flourishes. But we demand other things from civilization besides these, and it is a noticeable fact that we hope to find them realized in these same countries. As though we were seeking to repudiate the first demand we made, we welcome it as a sign of civilization as well if we see people directing their care too to what has no practical value whatever, to what is useless—if, for instance, the green spaces necessary in a town as playgrounds and as reservoirs of fresh air are also laid out with flower-beds, or if the windows of the houses are decorated with pots of flowers. We soon observe that this useless thing which we expect civilization to value is beauty. We require civilized man to reverence beauty wherever he sees it in nature and to create it in the objects of his handiwork so far as he is able. But this is far from exhausting our demands on civilization. We expect besides to see the signs of cleanliness and order. We do not think highly of the cultural level of an English country town in Shakespeare's time when we read that there was a big dung-heap in front of his father's house in Stratford; we are indignant and call it 'barbarous' (which is the opposite of civilized) when we find the paths in the Wiener Wald[5] littered with paper. Dirtiness of any kind seems to us incompatible with civilization. We extend our demand for cleanliness to the human body too. We are astonished to learn of the objectionable smell which emanated from the *Roi Soleil*;[6] and we shake our heads on

[5] [The wooded hills on the outskirts of Vienna.]
[6] [Louis XIV of France.]

the Isola Bella[7] when we are shown the tiny wash-basin in which Napoleon made his morning toilet. Indeed, we are not surprised by the idea of setting up the use of soap as an actual yardstick of civilization. The same is true of order. It, like cleanliness, applies solely to the works of man. But whereas cleanliness is not to be expected in nature, order, on the contrary, has been imitated from her. Man's observation of the great astronomical regularities not only furnished him with a model for introducing order into his life, but gave him the first points of departure for doing so. Order is a kind of compulsion to repeat which, when a regulation has been laid down once and for all, decides when, where and how a thing shall be done, so that in every similar circumstance one is spared hesitation and indecision. The benefits of order are incontestable. It enables men to use space and time to the best advantage, while conserving their psychical forces. We should have a right to expect that order would have taken its place in human activities from the start and without difficulty; and we may well wonder that this has not happened—that, on the contrary, human beings exhibit an inborn tendency to carelessness, irregularity and unreliability in their work, and that a laborious training is needed before they learn to follow the example of their celestial models.

Beauty, cleanliness and order obviously occupy a special

[7] [The well-known island in Lake Maggiore, visited by Napoleon a few days before the battle of Marengo.]

position among the requirements of civilization. No one will maintain that they are as important for life as control over the forces of nature or as some other factors with which we shall become acquainted. And yet no one would care to put them in the background as trivialities. That civilization is not exclusively taken up with what is useful is already shown by the example of beauty, which we decline to omit from among the interests of civilization. The usefulness of order is quite evident. With regard to cleanliness, we must bear in mind that it is demanded of us by hygiene as well, and we may suspect that even before the days of scientific prophylaxis the connection between the two was not altogether strange to man. Yet utility does not entirely explain these efforts; something else must be at work besides

No feature, however, seems better to characterize civilization than its esteem and encouragement of man's higher mental activities—his intellectual, scientific and artistic achievements—and the leading role that it assigns to ideas in human life. Foremost among those ideas are the religious systems, on whose complicated structure I have endeavoured to throw light elsewhere.[8] Next come the speculations of philosophy; and finally what might be called man's 'ideals'—his ideas of a possible perfection of individuals, or of peoples or of the whole of humanity, and the demands he sets up on the basis of such ideas. The fact that these creations of his are not inde-

[8] [Cf. *The Future of an Illusion* (1927c).]

pendent of one another, but are on the contrary closely inter-
woven, increases the difficulty not only of describing them but
of tracing their psychological derivation. If we assume quite
generally that the motive force of all human activities is a striving towards the two confluent goals of utility and a yield of
pleasure, we must suppose that this is also true of the manifestations of civilization which we have been discussing here,
although this is easily visible only in scientific and aesthetic
activities. But it cannot be doubted that the other activities, too,
correspond to strong needs in men—perhaps to needs which
are only developed in a minority. Nor must we allow ourselves
to be misled by judgements of value concerning any particular
religion, or philosophic system, or ideal. Whether we think to
find in them the highest achievements of the human spirit, or
whether we deplore them as aberrations, we cannot but recognize that where they are present, and, in especial, where they
are dominant, a high level of civilization is implied.

The last, but certainly not the least important, of the characteristic features of civilization remains to be assessed: the
manner in which the relationships of men to one another, their
social relationships, are regulated—relationships which affect a
person as a neighbour, as a source of help, as another person's
sexual object, as a member of a family and of a State. Here it is
especially difficult to keep clear of particular ideal demands
and to see what is civilized in general. Perhaps we may begin
by explaining that the element of civilization enters on the
scene with the first attempt to regulate these social relation-

ships. If the attempt were not made, the relationships would be subject to the arbitrary will of the individual; that is to say, the physically stronger man would decide them in the sense of his own interests and instinctual impulses. Nothing would be changed in this if this stronger man should in his turn meet someone even stronger than he. Human life in common is only made possible when a majority comes together which is stronger than any separate individual and which remains united against all separate individuals. The power of this community is then set up as 'right' in opposition to the power of the individual, which is condemned as 'brute force'. This replacement of the power of the individual by the power of a community constitutes the decisive step of civilization. The essence of it lies in the fact that the members of the community restrict themselves in their possibilities of satisfaction, whereas the individual knew no such restrictions. The first requisite of civilization, therefore, is that of justice—that is, the assurance that a law once made will not be broken in favour of an individual. This implies nothing as to the ethical value of such a law. The further course of cultural development seems to tend towards making the law no longer an expression of the will of a small community—a caste or a stratum of the population or a racial group—which, in its turn, behaves like a violent individual towards other, and perhaps more numerous, collections of people. The final outcome should be a rule of law to which all—except those who are not capable of entering a community—have contributed by a sacrifice of their instincts, and which leaves no one—again with the same exception—at the mercy of brute force.

The liberty of the individual is no gift of civilization. It was greatest before there was any civilization, though then, it is true, it had for the most part no value, since the individual was scarcely in a position to defend it. The development of civilization imposes restrictions on it, and justice demands that no one shall escape those restrictions. What makes itself felt in a human community as a desire for freedom may be their revolt against some existing injustice, and so may prove favourable to a further development of civilization; it may remain compatible with civilization. But it may also spring from the remains of their original personality, which is still untamed by civilization and may thus become the basis in them of hostility to civilization.⌋The urge for freedom, therefore, is directed against particular forms and demands of civilization or against civilization altogether. It does not seem as though any influence could induce a man to change his nature into a termite's. No doubt he will always defend his claim to individual liberty against the will of the group. A good part of the struggles of mankind centre round the single task of finding an expedient accommodation— one, that is, that will bring happiness—between this claim of the individual and the cultural claims of the group; and one of the problems that touches the fate of humanity is whether such an accommodation can be reached by means of some particular form of civilization or whether this conflict is irreconcilable.

By allowing common feeling to be our guide in deciding

what features of human life are to be regarded as civilized, we have obtained a clear impression of the general picture of civilization; but it is true that so far we have discovered nothing that is not universally known. At the same time we have been careful not to fall in with the prejudice that civilization is synonymous with perfecting, that it is the road to perfection preordained for men. But now a point of view presents itself which may lead in a different direction. The development of civilization appears to us as a peculiar process which mankind undergoes, and in which several things strike us as familiar. We may characterize this process with reference to the changes which it brings about in the familiar instinctual dispositions of human beings, to satisfy which is, after all, the economic task of our lives. A few of these instincts are used up in such a manner that something appears in their place which, in an individual, we describe as a character-trait. The most remarkable example of such a process is found in the anal erotism of young human beings. Their original interest in the excretory function, its organs and products, is changed in the course of their growth into a group of traits which are familiar to us as parsimony, a sense of order and cleanliness—qualities which, though valuable and welcome in themselves, may be intensified till they become markedly dominant and produce what is called the anal character. How this happens we do not know, but there is no doubt about the correctness of the finding.[9] Now we have

[9] Cf. my 'Character and Anal Erotism' (1908*b*), and numerous further contributions, by Ernest Jones [1918] and others.

seen that order and cleanliness are important requirements of civilization, although their vital necessity is not very apparent, any more than their suitability as sources of enjoyment. At this point we cannot fail to be struck by the similarity between the process of civilization and the libidinal development of the individual. Other instincts [besides anal erotism] are induced to displace the conditions for their satisfaction, to lead them into other paths. In most cases this process coincides with that of the *sublimation* (of instinctual aims) with which we are familiar, but in some it can be differentiated from it. Sublimation of instinct is an especially conspicuous feature of cultural development; it is what makes it possible for higher psychical activities, scientific, artistic or ideological, to play such an important part in civilized life. If one were to yield to a first impression, one would say that sublimation is a vicissitude which has been forced upon the instincts entirely by civilization. But it would be wiser to reflect upon this a little longer. In the third place,[10] finally, and this seems the most important of all, it is impossible to overlook the extent to which civilization is built up upon a renunciation of instinct, how much it presupposes precisely the non-satisfaction (by suppression, repression or some other means?) of powerful instincts. This 'cultural frustration' dominates the large field of social relationships between human beings. As we already know, it is the cause of the hostility

---

[10] [Freud had already mentioned two other factors playing a part in the 'process' of civilization: character-formation and sublimation.]

against which all civilizations have to struggle. It will also make severe demands on our scientific work, and we shall have much to explain here. It is not easy to understand how it can become possible to deprive an instinct of satisfaction. Nor is doing so without danger. If the loss is not compensated for economically, one can be certain that serious disorders will ensue.

But if we want to know what value can be attributed to our view that the development of civilization is a special process, comparable to the normal maturation of the individual, we must clearly attack another problem. We must ask ourselves to what influences the development of civilization owes its origin, how it arose, and by what its course has been determined.[11]

---

[11] [Freud returns to the subject of civilization as a 'process' below, on p. 119 and again on p. 137. He mentions it once more in his open letter to Einstein, *Why War?* (1933b).]

IV

THE TASK SEEMS an immense one, and it is natural to feel diffidence in the face of it. But here are such conjectures as I have been able to make.

After primal man had discovered that it lay in his own hands, literally, to improve his lot on earth by working, it cannot have been a matter of indifference to him whether another man worked with or against him. The other man acquired the value for him of a fellow-worker, with whom it was useful to live together. Even earlier, in his ape-like prehistory, man had adopted the habit of forming families, and the members of his family were probably his first helpers. One may suppose that the founding of families was connected with the fact that a moment came when the need for genital satisfaction no longer made its appearance like a guest who drops in suddenly, and, after his departure, is heard of no more for a long time, but instead took up its quarters as a permanent lodger. When this happened, the male acquired a motive for keeping the female, or, speaking more generally, his sexual objects, near him; while the female, who did not want to be separated from her helpless young, was obliged, in their interests, to remain with the stronger male.[1] In this primitive family one essential feature of

[1] The organic periodicity of the sexual process has persisted, it is true, but its effect on psychical sexual excitation has rather been reversed. This change seems most likely to be connected with the diminution of the olfactory stimuli by means of which the menstrual process produced an effect on the male psyche. Their role was taken over by visual excitations, which, in contrast to the intermittent olfactory stimuli, were able to maintain a permanent effect. The taboo on menstruation is derived from this 'organic repression', as a defence against a phase of development that has been surmounted. All other motives are probably of a secondary nature. (Cf. C. D. Daly, 1927.) This process is repeated on another level when the gods of a superseded period of civilization turn into demons. The diminution of the olfactory stimuli seems itself to be a consequence of man's raising himself from the ground, of his assumption of an upright gait; this made his genitals, which were previously concealed, visible and in need of protection, and so provoked feelings of shame in him.

The fateful process of civilization would thus have set in with man's adoption of an erect posture. From that point the chain of events would have proceeded through the devaluation of olfactory stimuli and the isolation of the menstrual period to the time when visual stimuli were paramount and the genitals became visible, and thence to the continuity of sexual excitation, the founding of the family and so to the threshold of human civilization. This is only a theoretical speculation, but it is important enough to deserve careful checking with reference to the conditions of life which obtain among animals closely related to man.

A social factor is also unmistakably present in the cultural trend towards cleanliness, which has received *ex post facto* justification in hygienic considerations but which manifested itself before their discovery. The incitement to cleanliness originates in an urge to get rid of the excreta, which have become disagreeable to the sense perceptions. We know that in the nursery things are different. The excreta arouse no disgust in children. They seem valuable to them as being a part of their own body which has come away from it. Here upbringing insists with special energy on hastening the course of development which lies ahead, and which should

civilization is still lacking. The arbitrary will of its head, the father, was unrestricted. In *Totem and Taboo* [1912–13][2] I have tried to show how the way led from this family to the succeeding stage of communal life in the form of bands of brothers. In overpowering their father, the sons had made the discovery that a combination can be stronger than a single individual. The totemic culture is based on the restrictions which the sons had to impose on one another in order to keep this new state of affairs in being. The taboo-observances were the first 'right' or 'law'.[3] The communal life of human beings had, therefore, a two-fold foundation: the compulsion to work, which was created by external necessity, and the power of love, which made

---

make the excreta worthless, disgusting, abhorrent and abominable. Such a reversal of values would scarcely be possible if the substances that are expelled from the body were not doomed by their strong smells to share the fate which overtook olfactory stimuli after man adopted the erect posture. Anal erotism, therefore, succumbs in the first instance to the 'organic repression' which paved the way to civilization. The existence of the social factor which is responsible for the further transformation of anal erotism is attested by the circumstance that, in spite of all man's developmental advances, he scarcely finds the smell of *his own* excreta repulsive, but only that of other people's. Thus a person who is not clean—who does not hide his excreta—is offending other people; he is showing no consideration for them. And this is confirmed by our strongest and commonest terms of abuse. It would be incomprehensible, too, that man should use the name of his most faithful friend in the animal world—the dog—as a term of abuse if that creature had not incurred his contempt through two characteristics: that it is an animal whose dominant sense is that of smell and one which has no horror of excrement, and that it is not ashamed of its sexual functions.

[2] [What Freud here calls the 'primitive family' he speaks of more often as the 'primal horde'; it corresponds to what Atkinson (1903), to whom the notion is largely due, named the 'Cyclopean family'.]

[3] [The German *'Recht'* means both 'right' and 'law'.]

the man unwilling to be deprived of his sexual object—the woman—, and made the woman unwilling to be deprived of the part of herself which had been separated off from her—her child. Eros and Ananke [Love and Necessity] have become the parents of human civilization too. The first result of civilization was that even a fairly large number of people were now able to live together in a community. And since these two great powers were cooperating in this, one might expect that the further development of civilization would proceed smoothly towards an even better control over the external world and towards a further extension of the number of people included in the community. Nor is it easy to understand how this civilization could act upon its participants otherwise than to make them happy.

Before we go on to enquire from what quarter an interference might arise, this recognition of love as one of the foundations of civilization may serve as an excuse for a digression which will enable us to fill in a gap which we left in an earlier discussion [p. 63]. We said there that man's discovery that sexual (genital) love afforded him the strongest experiences of satisfaction, and in fact provided him with the prototype of all happiness, must have suggested to him that he should continue to seek the satisfaction of happiness in his life along the path of sexual relations and that he should make genital erotism the central point of his life. We went on to say that in doing so he made himself dependent in a most dangerous way on a portion of the external world, namely, his chosen love-object, and exposed himself to extreme suffering if he should be rejected by that object or should lose it through unfaithfulness or death. For that reason the wise men of every age have warned us most emphatically against this way of life; but in spite of this it has not lost its attraction for a great number of people.

A small minority are enabled by their constitution to find happiness, in spite of everything, along the path of love. But far-reaching mental changes in the function of love are necessary before this can happen. These people make themselves independent of their object's acquiescence by displacing what they mainly value from being loved on to loving; they protect themselves against the loss of the object by directing their love, not to single objects but to all men alike; and they avoid the uncertainties and disappointments of genital love by turning away from its sexual aims and transforming the instinct into an impulse with an *inhibited aim*. What they bring about in themselves in this way is a state of evenly suspended, steadfast, affectionate feeling, which has little external resemblance any more to the stormy agitations of genital love, from which it is nevertheless derived. Perhaps St. Francis of Assisi went furthest in thus exploiting love for the benefit of an inner feeling of happiness. Moreover, what we have recognized as one of the techniques for fulfilling the pleasure principle has often been brought into connection with religion; this connection may lie in the remote regions where the distinction between the ego and objects or between objects themselves is neglected. According to one ethical view, whose deeper motivation will become clear to us presently, this readiness for a universal love of mankind and the world represents the highest standpoint which man can reach. Even at this early stage of the discussion I should like to bring forward my two main objections to this view. A love that does not discriminate seems to me to forfeit a part of its own value, by doing an injustice to its object; and secondly, not all men are worthy of love.

The love which founded the family continues to operate in civilization both in its original form, in which it does not renounce direct sexual satisfaction, and in its modified form as aim-inhibited affection. In each, it continues to carry on its function of binding together considerable numbers of people, and it does so in a more intensive fashion than can be effected through the interest of work in common. The careless way in which language uses the word 'love' has its genetic justification. People give the name 'love' to the relation between a man and a woman whose genital needs have led them to found a family; but they also give the name 'love' to the positive feelings between parents and children, and between the brothers and sisters of a family, although *we* are obliged to describe this as 'aim-inhibited love' or 'affection'. Love with an inhibited aim was in fact originally fully sensual love, and it is so still in man's unconscious. Both—fully sensual love and aim-inhibited love—extend outside the family and create new bonds with people who before were strangers. Genital love leads to the formation of new families, and aim-inhibited love to 'friendships' which become valuable from a cultural standpoint because they escape some of the limitations of genital love, as, for instance, its exclusiveness. But in the course of development the relation of love to civilization loses its unambiguity. On the one hand love comes into opposition to the interests of civilization; on the other, civilization threatens love with substantial restrictions.

This rift between them seems unavoidable. The reason for it is not immediately recognizable. It expresses itself at first as a conflict between the family and the larger community to which the individual belongs. We have already perceived that one of the main endeavours of civilization is to bring people together into large unities. But the family will not give the individual up. The more closely the members of a family are attached to one another, the more often do they tend to cut themselves off from others, and the more difficult is it for them to enter into the wider circle of life. The mode of life in common which is phylogenetically the older, and which is the only one that exists in childhood, will not let itself be superseded by the cultural mode of life which has been acquired later. Detaching himself from his family becomes a task that faces every young person, and society often helps him in the solution of it by means of puberty and initiation rites. We get the impression that these are difficulties which are inherent in all psychical—and, indeed, at bottom, in all organic—development.

Furthermore, women soon come into opposition to civilization and display their retarding and restraining influence—those very women who, in the beginning, laid the foundations of civilization by the claims of their love. Women represent the interests of the family and of sexual life. The work of civilization has become increasingly the business of men, it confronts them with ever more difficult tasks and compels them to carry out instinctual sublimations of which women are little capable. Since a man does not have unlimited quantities of psychical energy at his disposal, he has to accomplish his tasks by making an expedient distribution of his libido. What he employs for cultural aims he to a great extent withdraws from women and sexual life. His constant association with men, and his dependence on his relations with them, even estrange him from his duties as a husband and father. Thus the woman finds herself forced into the background by the claims of civilization and she adopts a hostile attitude towards it.

The tendency on the part of civilization to restrict sexual life is no less clear than its other tendency to expand the cultural unit. Its first, totemic, phase already brings with it the prohibition against an incestuous choice of object, and this is perhaps the most drastic mutilation which man's erotic life has in all time experienced. Taboos, laws and customs impose further restrictions, which affect both men and women. Not all civilizations go equally far in this; and the economic structure of the society also influences the amount of sexual freedom that remains. Here, as we already know, civilization is obeying the laws of economic necessity, since a large amount of the psychical energy which it uses for its own purposes has to be withdrawn from sexuality. In this respect civilization behaves towards sexuality as a people or a stratum of its population does which has subjected another one to its exploitation. Fear of a revolt by the suppressed elements drives it to stricter precautionary measures. A high-water mark in such a development has been reached in our Western European civilization. A cultural community is perfectly justified, psychologically, in starting by proscribing manifestations of the sexual life of children, for there would be no prospect of curbing the sexual lusts of adults if the ground had not been prepared for it in childhood. But such a community cannot in any way be justified in going to the length of actually *disavowing* such easily demonstrable, and, indeed, striking phenomena. As regards the sexually mature individual, the choice of an object is restricted to the opposite sex, and most extra-genital satisfactions are forbidden as perversions. The requirement, demonstrated in these prohibitions, that there shall be a single kind of sexual life for everyone, disregards the dissimilarities, whether innate or acquired, in the sexual constitution of human beings; it cuts off a fair number of them from sexual enjoyment, and so becomes the source of serious injustice. The result of such restrictive measures might be that in people who are normal—who are not prevented by their constitution—the whole of their sexual interests would flow without loss into the channels that are left open. But heterosexual genital love, which has remained exempt from outlawry, is itself restricted by further limitations, in the shape of insistence upon legitimacy and monogamy. Present-day civilization makes it plain that it will only permit sexual relationships on the basis of a solitary, indissoluble bond between one man and one woman, and that it does not like sexuality as a source of pleasure in its own right and is only prepared to tolerate it because there is so far no substitute for it as a means of propagating the human race.

This, of course, is an extreme picture. Everybody knows that it has proved impossible to put it into execution, even for quite short periods.' Only the weaklings have submitted to such an extensive encroachment upon their sexual freedom, and stronger natures have only done so subject to a compensatory condition, which will be mentioned later. Civilized society has found itself obliged to pass over in silence many transgressions which, according to its own rescripts, it ought to have punished. But we must not err on the other side and assume that, because it does not achieve all its aims, such an attitude on the part of society is entirely innocuous. The sexual life of civilized man is notwithstanding severely impaired; it sometimes gives the impression of being in process of involution as a function, just as our teeth and hair seem to be as organs. One is probably justified in assuming that its importance as a source of feelings of happiness, and therefore in the fulfilment of our aim in life, has sensibly diminished.⁴ Sometimes one seems to per-

---

⁴ Among the works of that sensitive English writer, John Galsworthy, who enjoys general recognition to-day, there is a short story of which I early formed a high opinion. It is called 'The Apple-Tree', and it brings home to us how the life of present-day civilized people leaves no room for the simple natural love of two human beings.

ceive that it is not only the pressure of civilization but something in the nature of the function itself which denies us full satisfaction and urges us along other paths. This may be wrong; it is hard to decide.[5]

[5] The view expressed above is supported by the following considerations. Man is an animal organism with (like others) an unmistakably bisexual disposition. The individual corresponds to a fusion of two symmetrical halves, of which, according to some investigators, one is purely male and the other female. It is equally possible that each half was originally hermaphrodite. Sex is a biological fact which, although it is of extraordinary importance in mental life, is hard to grasp psychologically. We are accustomed to say that every human being displays both male and female instinctual impulses, needs and attributes; but though anatomy, it is true, can point out the characteristic of maleness and femaleness, psychology cannot. For psychology the contrast between the sexes fades away into one between activity and passivity, in which we far too readily identify activity with maleness and passivity with femaleness, a view which is by no means universally confirmed in the animal kingdom. The theory of bisexuality is still surrounded by many obscurities and we cannot but feel it as a serious impediment in psychoanalysis that it has not yet found any link with the theory of the instincts. However this may be, if we assume it as a fact that each individual seeks to satisfy both male and female wishes in his sexual life, we are prepared for the possibility that those [two sets of] demands are not fulfilled by the same object, and that they interfere with each other unless they can be kept apart and each impulse guided into a particular channel that is suited to it. Another difficulty arises from the circumstance that there is so often associated with the erotic relationship, over and above its own sadistic components, a quota of plain inclination to aggression. The love-object will not always view these complications with the degree of understanding and tolerance shown by the peasant woman who complained that her husband did not love her any more, since he had not beaten her for a week.

The conjecture which goes deepest, however, is the one which takes its start from what I have said above in my footnote on p. 87f. It is to the effect that, with the assumption of an erect posture by man and with the depreciation of his sense of smell, it was not only his anal erotism which threatened to fall a victim to organic repression, but the whole of his sexuality; so that since this, the sexual function has been accompanied by a repugnance which cannot further be accounted for, and

---

which prevents its complete satisfaction and forces it away from the sexual aim into sublimations and libidinal displacements. I know that Bleuler (1913) once pointed to the existence of a primary repelling attitude like this towards sexual life. All neurotics, and many others besides, take exception to the fact that *'inter urinas et faeces nascimur* [we are born between urine and faeces]'. The genitals, too, give rise to strong sensations of smell which many people cannot tolerate and which spoil sexual intercourse for them. Thus we should find that the deepest root of the sexual repression which advances along with civilization is the organic defence of the new form of life achieved with man's erect gait against his earlier animal existence. This result of scientific research coincides in a remarkable way with commonplace prejudices that have often made themselves heard. Nevertheless, these things are at present no more than unconfirmed possibilities which have not been substantiated by science. Nor should we forget that, in spite of the undeniable depreciation of olfactory stimuli, there exist even in Europe peoples among whom the strong genital odours which are so repellent to us are highly prized as sexual stimulants and who refuse to give them up. (Cf. the collections of folklore obtained from Iwan Bloch's questionnaire on the sense of smell in sexual life [*'Über den Geruchssinn in der vita sexualis'*] published in different volumes of Friedrich S. Krauss's *Anthropophyteia.*)

V

―

Psycho-analytic work has shown us that it is precisely these frustrations of sexual life which people known as neurotics cannot tolerate. The neurotic creates substitutive satisfactions for himself in his symptoms, and these either cause him suffering in themselves or become sources of suffering for him by raising difficulties in his relations with his environment and the society he belongs to. The latter fact is easy to understand; the former presents us with a new problem. But civilization demands other sacrifices besides that of sexual satisfaction.

We have treated the difficulty of cultural development as a general difficulty of development by tracing it to the inertia of the libido, to its disinclination to give up an old position for a new one. We are saying much the same thing when we derive the antithesis between civilization and sexuality from the circumstances that sexual love is a relationship between two individuals in which a third can only be superfluous or disturbing, whereas civilization depends on relationships between a considerable number of individuals. When a love-relationship is at its height there is no room left for any interest in the environment; a pair of lovers are sufficient to themselves, and do not even need the child they have in common to make them happy. In no other case does Eros so clearly betray the core of his being, his purpose of making one out of more than one; but when he has achieved this in the proverbial way through the love of two human beings, he refuses to go further.

So far, we can quite well imagine a cultural community consisting of double individuals like this, who, libidinally satisfied in themselves, are connected with one another through the bonds of common work and common interests. If this were so, civilization would not have to withdraw any energy from sexuality. But this desirable state of things does not, and never did, exist. Reality shows us that civilization is not content with the ties we have so far allowed it. It aims at binding the members of the community together in a libidinal way as well and employs every means to that end. It favours every path by which strong identifications can be established between the members of the community, and it summons up aim-inhibited libido on the largest scale so as to strengthen the communal bond by relations of friendship. In order for these aims to be fulfilled, a restriction upon sexual life is unavoidable. But we are unable to understand what the necessity is which forces civilization along this path and which causes its antagonism to sexuality. There must be some disturbing factor which we have not yet discovered.

The clue may be supplied by one of the ideal demands, as we have called them,[1] of civilized society. It runs: 'Thou shalt love thy neighbour as thyself.' It is known throughout the world and is undoubtedly older than Christianity, which puts it forward as its proudest claim. Yet it is certainly not very old; even in historical times it was still strange to mankind. Let us adopt a naïve attitude towards it, as though we were hearing it for the first time; we shall be unable then to suppress a feeling of surprise and bewilderment. Why should we do it? What good will it do us? But, above all, how shall we achieve it? How can it be possible? My love is something valuable to me which I ought not to throw away without reflection. It imposes duties on me for whose fulfilment I must be ready to make sacrifices. If I love someone, he must deserve it in some way. (I leave out of account the use he may be to me, and also his possible significance for me as a sexual object, for neither of these two kinds of relationship comes into question where the precept to love my neighbour is concerned.) He deserves it if he is so like me in important ways that I can love myself in him; and he deserves it if he is so much more perfect than myself that I can love my ideal of my own self in him. Again, I have to love him if he is my friend's son, since the pain my friend would feel if

[1] [See p. 151.]

CIVILIZATION AND ITS DISCONTENTS

any harm came to him would be my pain too—I should have to share it. But if he is a stranger to me and if he cannot attract me by any worth of his own or any significance that he may already have acquired for my emotional life, it will be hard for me to love him. Indeed, I should be wrong to do so, for my love is valued by all my own people as a sign of my preferring them, and it is an injustice to them if I put a stranger on a par with them. But if I am to love him (with this universal love) merely because he, too, is an inhabitant of this earth, like an insect, an earth-worm or a grass-snake, then I fear that only a small modicum of my love will fall to his share—not by any possibility as much as, by the judgement of my reason, I am entitled to retain for myself. What is the point of a precept enunciated with so much solemnity if its fulfilment cannot be recommended as reasonable?

On closer inspection, I find still further difficulties. Not merely is this stranger in general unworthy of my love; I must honestly confess that he has more claim to my hostility and even my hatred. He seems not to have the least trace of love for me and shows me not the slightest consideration. If it will do him any good he has no hesitation in injuring me, nor does he ask himself whether the amount of advantage he gains bears any proportion to the extent of the harm he does to me. Indeed, he need not even obtain an advantage; if he can satisfy any sort of desire by it, he thinks nothing of jeering at me, insulting me, slandering me and showing his superior power; and the more secure he feels and the more helpless I am, the more certainly I can expect him to behave like this to me. If he behaves differently, if he shows me consideration and forbearance as a stranger, I am ready to treat him in the same way, in any case and quite apart from any precept. Indeed, if this grandiose commandment had run 'Love thy neighbour as thy neighbour loves thee', I should not take exception to it. And there is a second commandment, which seems to me even more incomprehensible and arouses still stronger opposition in me. It is 'Love thine enemies'. If I think it over, however, I see that I am wrong in treating it as a greater imposition. At bottom it is the same thing.[2]

I think I can now hear a dignified voice admonishing me: 'It is precisely because your neighbour is not worthy of love, and is on the contrary your enemy, that you should love him as yourself.' I then understand that the case is one like that of *Credo quia absurdum*.[3]

Now it is very probable that my neighbour, when he is

[2] A great imaginative writer may permit himself to give expression—jokingly, at all events—to psychological truths that are severely proscribed. Thus Heine confesses: 'Mine is a most peaceable disposition. My wishes are: a humble cottage with a thatched roof, but a good bed, good food, the freshest milk and butter, flowers before my window, and a few fine trees before my door; and if God wants to make my happiness complete, he will grant me the joy of seeing some six or seven of my enemies hanging from those trees. Before their death I shall, moved in my heart, forgive them all the wrong they did me in their lifetime. One must, it is true, forgive one's enemies—but not before they have been hanged.' (*Gedanken und Einfälle* [Section I].)

[3] [Freud returns to the question of the commandment to love one's neighbour as oneself below, on p. 151f.]

CIVILIZATION AND ITS DISCONTENTS

enjoined to love me as himself, will answer exactly as I have done and will repel me for the same reasons. I hope he will not have the same objective grounds for doing so, but he will have the same idea as I have. Even so, the behaviour of human beings shows differences, which ethics, disregarding the fact that such differences are determined, classifies as 'good' or 'bad'. So long as these undeniable differences have not been removed, obedience to high ethical demands entails damage to the aims of civilization, for it puts a positive premium on being bad. One is irresistibly reminded of an incident in the French Chamber when capital punishment was being debated. A member had been passionately supporting its abolition and his speech was being received with tumultuous applause, when a voice from the hall called out: 'Que messieurs les assassins commencent!'[4]

The element of truth behind all this, which people are so ready to disavow, is that men are not gentle creatures who want to be loved, and who at the most can defend themselves if they are attacked; they are, on the contrary, creatures among whose instinctual endowments is to be reckoned a powerful share of aggressiveness. As a result, their neighbour is for them not only a potential helper or sexual object, but also someone who tempts them to satisfy their aggressiveness on him, to exploit his capacity for work without compensation, to use him sexually without his consent, to seize his possessions, to humil-

[4] ['It's the murderers who should make the first move.']   68

iate him, to cause him pain, to torture and to kill him. *Homo homini lupus.*[5] Who, in the face of all his experience of life and of history, will have the courage to dispute this assertion? As a rule this cruel aggressiveness waits for some provocation or puts itself at the service of some other purpose, whose goal might also have been reached by milder measures. In circumstances that are favourable to it, when the mental counter-forces which ordinarily inhibit it are out of action, it also manifests itself spontaneously and reveals man as a savage beast to whom consideration towards his own kind is something alien. Anyone who calls to mind the atrocities committed during the racial migrations or the invasions of the Huns, or by the people known as Mongols under Jenghiz Khan and Tamerlane, or at the capture of Jerusalem by the pious Crusaders, or even, indeed, the horrors of the recent World War—anyone who calls these things to mind will have to bow humbly before the truth of this view.

The existence of this inclination to aggression, which we can detect in ourselves and justly assume to be present in others, is the factor which disturbs our relations with our neighbour and which forces civilization into such a high expenditure [of energy]. In consequence of this primary mutual hostility of human beings, civilized society is perpetually threatened with disintegration. The interest of work in common would not hold it together; instinctual passions are stronger than reason-

[5] ['Man is a wolf to man.' Derived from Plautus, *Asinaria* II, iv, 88.]

able interests. Civilization has to use its utmost efforts in order to set limits to man's aggressive instincts and to hold the manifestations of them in check by psychical reaction-formations. Hence, therefore, the use of methods intended to incite people into identifications and aim-inhibited relationships of love, hence the restriction upon sexual life, and hence too the ideal's commandment to love one's neighbour as oneself—a commandment which is really justified by the fact that nothing else runs so strongly counter to the original nature of man. In spite of every effort, these endeavours of civilization have not so far achieved very much. It hopes to prevent the crudest excesses of brutal violence by itself assuming the right to use violence against criminals, but the law is not able to lay hold of the more cautious and refined manifestations of human aggressiveness. The time comes when each one of us has to give up as illusions the expectations which, in his youth, he pinned upon his fellow-men, and when he may learn how much difficulty and pain has been added to his life by their ill-will. At the same time, it would be unfair to reproach civilization with trying to eliminate strife and competition from human activity. These things are undoubtedly indispensable. But opposition is not necessarily enmity; it is merely misused and made an *occasion* for enmity.

The communists believe that they have found the path to deliverance from our evils. According to them, man is wholly good and is well-disposed to his neighbour; but the institution of private property has corrupted his nature. The ownership of private wealth gives the individual power, and with it the temptation to ill-treat his neighbour; while the man who is excluded from possession is bound to rebel in hostility against his oppressor. If private property were abolished, all wealth held in common, and everyone allowed to share in the enjoyment of it, ill-will and hostility would disappear among men. Since everyone's needs would be satisfied, no one would have any reason to regard another as his enemy; all would willingly undertake the work that was necessary. I have no concern with any economic criticisms of the communist system; I cannot enquire into whether the abolition of private property is expedient or advantageous.[6] But I am able to recognize that the psychological premisses on which the system is based are an untenable illusion. In abolishing private property we deprive the human love of aggression of one of its instruments, certainly a strong one, though certainly not the strongest; but we have in no way altered the differences in power and influence which are misused by aggressiveness, nor have we altered anything in its nature. Aggressiveness was not created by property. It reigned almost without limit in primitive times, when prop-

---

[6] Anyone who has tasted the miseries of poverty in his own youth and has experienced the indifference and arrogance of the well-to-do, should be safe from the suspicion of having no understanding or good will towards endeavours to fight against the inequality of wealth among men and all that it leads to. To be sure, if an attempt is made to base this fight upon an abstract demand, in the name of justice, for equality for all men, there is a very obvious objection to be made—that nature, by endowing individuals with extremely unequal physical attributes and mental capacities, has introduced injustices against which there is no remedy.

erty was still very scanty, and it already shows itself in the nursery almost before property has given up its primal, anal form; it forms the basis of every relation of affection and love among people (with the single exception, perhaps, of the mother's relation to her male child). If we do away with personal rights over material wealth, there still remains prerogative in the field of sexual relationships, which is bound to become the source of the strongest dislike and the most violent hostility among men who in other respects are on an equal footing. If we were to remove this factor, too, by allowing complete freedom of sexual life and thus abolishing the family, the germ-cell of civilization, we cannot, it is true, easily foresee what new paths the development of civilization could take; but one thing we can expect, and that is that this indestructible feature of human nature will follow it there.

It is clearly not easy for men to give up the satisfaction of this inclination to aggression. They do not feel comfortable without it. The advantage which a comparatively small cultural group offers of allowing this instinct an outlet in the form of hostility against intruders is not to be despised. It is always possible to bind together a considerable number of people in love, so long as there are other people left over to receive the manifestations of their aggressiveness. I once discussed the phenomenon that it is precisely communities with adjoining territories, and related to each other in other ways as well, who are engaged in constant feuds and in ridiculing each other— like the Spaniards and Portuguese, for instance, the North

Germans and South Germans, the English and Scotch, and so on. I gave this phenomenon the name of 'the narcissism of minor differences', a name which does not do much to explain it. We can now see that it is a convenient and relatively harmless satisfaction of the inclination to aggression, by means of which cohesion between the members of the community is made easier. In this respect the Jewish people, scattered everywhere, have rendered most useful services to the civilizations of the countries that have been their hosts; but unfortunately all the massacres of the Jews in the Middle Ages did not suffice to make that period more peaceful and secure for their Christian fellows. When once the Apostle Paul had posited universal love between men as the foundation of his Christian community, extreme intolerance on the part of Christendom towards those who remained outside it became the inevitable consequence. To the Romans, who had not founded their communal life as a State upon love, religious intolerance was something foreign, although with them religion was a concern of the State and the State was permeated by religion. Neither was it an unaccountable chance that the dream of a Germanic world-dominion called for antisemitism as its complement; and it is intelligible that the attempt to establish a new, communist civilization in Russia should find its psychological support in the persecution of the bourgeois. One only wonders, with concern, what the Soviets will do after they have wiped out their bourgeois.

If civilization imposes such great sacrifices not only on man's sexuality but on his aggressivity, we can understand better why it is hard for him to be happy in that civilization. In fact, primitive man was better off in knowing no restrictions of instinct. To counterbalance this, his prospects of enjoying this happiness for any length of time were very slender. Civilized man has exchanged a portion of his possibilities of happiness for a portion of security. We must not forget, however, that in the primal family only the head of it enjoyed this instinctual freedom; the rest lived in slavish suppression. In that primal period of civilization, the contrast between a minority who enjoyed the advantages of civilization and a majority who were robbed of those advantages was, therefore, carried to extremes. As regards the primitive peoples who exist to-day, careful researches have shown that their instinctual life is by no means to be envied for its freedom. It is subject to restrictions of a different kind but perhaps of greater severity than those attaching to modern civilized man.

When we justly find fault with the present state of our civilization for so inadequately fulfilling our demands for a plan of life that shall make us happy, and for allowing the existence of so much suffering which could probably be avoided—when, with unsparing criticism, we try to uncover the roots of its imperfection, we are undoubtedly exercising a proper right and are not showing ourselves enemies of civilization. We may expect gradually to carry through such alterations in our civilization as will better satisfy our needs and will escape our criticisms. But perhaps we may also familiarize ourselves with the idea that there are difficulties attaching to the nature of civilization which will not yield to any attempt at reform. Over and above the tasks of restricting the instincts, which we are prepared for, there forces itself on our notice the danger of a state of things which might be termed 'the psychological poverty of groups'. This danger is most threatening where the bonds of a society are chiefly constituted by the identification of its members with one another, while individuals of the leader type do not acquire the importance that should fall to them in the formation of a group.[7] The present cultural state of America would give us a good opportunity for studying the damage to civilization which is thus to be feared. But I shall avoid the temptation of entering upon a critique of American civilization; I do not wish to give an impression of wanting myself to employ American methods.

[7] f. *Group Psychology and the Analysis of the Ego* (1921c).

VI

In NONE OF my previous writings have I had so strong a feeling as now that what I am describing is common knowledge and that I am using up paper and ink and, in due course, the compositor's and printer's work and material in order to expound things which are, in fact, self-evident. For that reason I should be glad to seize the point if it were to appear that the recognition of a special, independent aggressive instinct means an alteration of the psycho-analytic theory of the instincts.

We shall see, however, that this is not so and that it is merely a matter of bringing into sharper focus a turn of thought arrived at long ago and of following out its consequences. Of all the slowly developed parts of analytic theory, the theory of the instincts is the one that has felt its way the most painfully forward. And yet that theory was so indispensable to the whole structure that something had to be put in its place. In what was at first my utter perplexity, I took as my starting-point a saying of the poet-philosopher, Schiller, that 'hunger and love are what moves the world'.[1] Hunger could be taken to represent the instincts which aim at preserving the individual; while love strives after objects, and its chief function, favoured in every way by nature, is the preservation of the species. Thus, to begin with, ego-instincts and object-instincts confronted each other. It was to denote the energy of the latter and only the latter instincts that I introduced the term 'libido'. Thus the antithesis was between the ego-instincts and the 'libidinal' instincts of love (in its widest sense) which were directed to an object. One of these object-instincts, the sadistic instinct, stood out from the rest, it is true, in that its aim was so very far from being loving. Moreover it was obviously in some respects attached to the ego-instincts: it could not hide its close affinity with instincts of mastery which have no libidinal purpose. But these discrepancies were got over; after all, sadism was clearly a part of sexual life, in the activities of which affection could be replaced by cruelty. Neurosis was regarded as the outcome of a struggle between the interest of self-preservation and the demands of the libido, a struggle in which the ego had been victorious but at the price of severe sufferings and renunciations.

Every analyst will admit that even to-day this view has not

[1] ['Die Weltweisen.']

the sound of a long-discarded error. Nevertheless, alterations in it became essential, as our enquiries advanced from the repressed to the repressing forces, from the object instincts to the ego. The decisive step forward was the introduction of the concept of narcissism—that is to say, the discovery that the ego itself is cathected with libido, that the ego, indeed, is the libido's original home, and remains to some extent its head-quarters. This narcissistic libido turns towards objects, and thus becomes object-libido; and it can change back into narcissistic libido once more. The concept of narcissism made it possible to obtain an analytic understanding of the traumatic neuroses and of many of the affections bordering on the psychoses, as well as of the latter themselves. It was not necessary to give up our interpretation of the transference neuroses as attempts made by the ego to defend itself against sexuality; but the concept of libido was endangered. Since the ego-instincts, too, were libidinal, it seemed for a time inevitable that we should make libido coincide with instinctual energy in general, as C. G. Jung had already advocated earlier. Nevertheless, there still remained in me a kind of conviction, for which I was not as yet able to find reasons, that the instincts could not all be of the same kind. My next step was taken in *Beyond the Pleasure Principle* (1920*g*), when the compulsion to repeat and the conservative character of instinctual life first attracted my attention. Starting from speculations on the beginning of life and from biological parallels, I drew the conclusion that, besides the instinct to preserve living substance and to join it into ever larger units,[2] there must exist another, contrary instinct seeking to dissolve those units and to bring them back to their primaeval, inorganic state. That is to say, as well as Eros there was an instinct of death. The phenomena of life could be explained from the concurrent or mutually opposing action of these two instincts. It was not easy, however, to demonstrate the activities of this supposed death instinct. The manifestations of Eros were conspicuous and noisy enough. It might be assumed that the death instinct operated silently within the organism towards its dissolution, but that, of course, was no proof. A more fruitful idea was that a portion of the instinct is diverted towards the external world and comes to light as an instinct of aggressiveness and destructiveness. In this way the instinct itself could be pressed into the service of Eros, in that the organism was destroying some other thing, whether animate or inanimate, instead of destroying its own self. Conversely, any restriction of this aggressiveness directed outwards would be bound to increase the self-destruction, which is in any case proceeding. At the same time one can suspect from this example that the two kinds of instinct seldom—perhaps never— appear in isolation from each other, but are alloyed with each other in varying and very different proportions and so become unrecognizable to our judgement. In sadism, long since known

---

[2] The opposition which thus emerges between the ceaseless trend by Eros towards extension and the general conservative nature of the instincts is striking, and it may become the starting-point for the study of further problems.

to us as a component instinct of sexuality, we should have before us a particularly strong alloy of this kind between trends of love and the destructive instinct; while its counterpart, masochism, would be a union between destructiveness directed inwards and sexuality—a union which makes what is otherwise an imperceptible trend into a conspicuous and tangible one.

The assumption of the existence of an instinct of death or destruction has met with resistance even in analytic circles; I am aware that there is a frequent inclination rather to ascribe whatever is dangerous and hostile in love to an original bipolarity in its own nature. To begin with it was only tentatively that I put forward the views I have developed here, but in the course of time they have gained such a hold upon me that I can no longer think in any other way. To my mind, they are far more serviceable from a theoretical standpoint than any other possible ones; they provide that simplification, without either ignoring or doing violence to the facts, for which we strive in scientific work. I know that in sadism and masochism we have always seen before us manifestations of the destructive instinct (directed outwards and inwards), strongly alloyed with erotism; but I can no longer understand how we can have overlooked the ubiquity of non-erotic aggressivity and destructiveness and can have failed to give it its due place in our interpretation of life. (The desire for destruction when it is directed *inwards* mostly eludes our perception, of course, unless it is tinged with erotism.) I remember my own defensive attitude when the idea of an instinct of destruction first emerged in psychoanalytic literature, and how long it took before I became receptive to it. That others should have shown, and still show, the same attitude of rejection surprises me less. For 'little children do not like it'[3] when there is talk of the inborn human inclination to 'badness', to aggressiveness and destructiveness, and so to cruelty as well. God has made them in the image of His own perfection; nobody wants to be reminded how hard it is to reconcile the undeniable existence of evil—despite the protestations of Christian Science—with His all-powerfulness or His all-goodness. The Devil would be the best way out as an excuse for God; in that way he would be playing the same part as an agent of economic discharge as the Jew does in the world of the Aryan ideal. But even so, one can hold God responsible for the existence of the Devil just as well as for the existence of the wickedness which the Devil embodies. In view of these difficulties, each of us will be well advised, on some suitable occasion, to make a low bow to the deeply moral nature of mankind; it will help us to be generally popular and much will be forgiven us for it.[4]

[3] ['Denn die Kindlein, Sie hören es nicht gerne.' A quotation from Goethe's poem 'Die Ballade vom vertriebenen und heimgekehrten Grafen'.]

[4] In Goethe's Mephistopheles we have a quite exceptionally convincing identification of the principle of evil with the destructive instinct:

> Denn alles, was entsteht,
> Ist wert, dass es zu Grunde geht . . .
> So ist dann alles, was Ihr Sünde,
> Zerstörung, kurz das Böse nennt,
> Mein eigentliches Element.

The name 'libido' can once more be used to denote the manifestations of the power of Eros in order to distinguish them from the energy of the death instinct.[5] It must be confessed that we have much greater difficulty in grasping that instinct; we can only suspect it, as it were, as something in the background behind Eros, and it escapes detection unless its presence is betrayed by its being alloyed with Eros. It is in sadism, where the death instinct twists the erotic aim in its own sense and yet at the same time fully satisfies the erotic urge, that we succeed in obtaining the clearest insight into its nature and its

---

[For all things, from the Void
Called forth, deserve to be destroyed . . .
Thus, all which you as Sin have rated—
Destruction,—aught with Evil blent,—
That is my proper element.]

The Devil himself names as his adversary, not what is holy and good, but Nature's power to create, to multiply life—that is, Eros:

Der Luft, dem Wasser, wie der Erden
Entwinden tausend Keime sich,
Im Trocknen, Feuchten, Warmen, Kalten!
Hätt' ich mir nicht die Flamme vorbehalten,
Ich hätte nichts Aparts für mich.

[From Water, Earth, and Air unfolding,
A thousand germs break forth and grow,
In dry, and wet, and warm, and chilly:
And had I not the Flame reserved, why, really,
There's nothing special of my own to show.

Both passages are from Goethe's *Faust*, Part I, Scene 3. Translated by Bayard Taylor.]
    [5] Our present point of view can be roughly expressed in the statement that libido has a share in every instinctual manifestation, but that not everything in that manifestation is libido.

relation to Eros. But even where it emerges without any sexual purpose, in the blindest fury of destructiveness, we cannot fail to recognize that the satisfaction of the instinct is accompanied by an extraordinarily high degree of narcissistic enjoyment, owing to its presenting the ego with a fulfilment of the latter's old wishes for omnipotence. The instinct of destruction, moderated and tamed, and, as it were, inhibited in its aim, must, when it is directed towards objects, provide the ego with the satisfaction of its vital needs and with control over nature. Since the assumption of the existence of the instinct is mainly based on theoretical grounds, we must also admit that it is not entirely proof against theoretical objections. But this is how things appear to us now, in the present state of our knowledge; future research and reflection will no doubt bring further light which will decide the matter.

In all that follows I adopt the standpoint, therefore, that the inclination to aggression is an original, self-subsisting instinctual disposition in man, and I return to my view [p. 104] that it constitutes the greatest impediment to civilization. At one point in the course of this enquiry [p. 83] I was led to the idea that civilization was a special process which mankind undergoes, and I am still under the influence of that idea. I may now add that civilization is a process in the service of Eros, whose purpose is to combine single human individuals, and after that families, then races, peoples and nations, into one great unity, the unity of mankind. Why this has to happen, we do not know; the work of Eros is precisely this. These collections of men are to be libidinally bound to one another. Necessity alone, the advantages of work in common, will not hold them together. But man's natural aggressive instinct, the hostility of each against all and of all against each, opposes this programme of civilization. This aggressive instinct is the derivative and the main representative of the death instinct which we have found alongside of Eros and which shares world-dominion with it. And now, I think, the meaning of the evolution of civilization is no longer obscure to us. It must present the struggle between Eros and Death, between the instinct of life and the instinct of destruction, as it works itself out in the human species. This struggle is what all life essentially consists of, and the evolution of civilization may therefore be simply described as the struggle for life of the human species.[6] And it is this battle of the giants that our nurse-maids try to appease with their lullaby about Heaven.[7]

---

[6] And we may probably add more precisely, a struggle for life in the shape it was bound to assume after a certain event which still remains to be discovered.

[7] ['Eiapopeia vom Himmel,' A quotation from Heine's poem Deutschland, Caput I.]

VII

WHY DO OUR relatives, the animals, not exhibit any such cultural struggle? We do not know. Very probably some of them—the bees, the ants, the termites—strove for thousands of years before they arrived at the State institutions, the distribution of functions and the restrictions on the individual, for which we admire them to-day. It is a mark of our present condition that we know from our own feelings that we should not think ourselves happy in any of these animal States or in any of the roles assigned in them to the individual. In the case of other animal species it may be that a temporary balance has been reached between the influences of their environment and the mutually contending instincts within them, and that thus a cessation of development has come about. It may be that in primitive man a fresh access of libido kindled a renewed burst of activity on the part of the destructive instinct. There are a great many questions here to which as yet there is no answer.

Another question concerns us more nearly. What means does civilization employ in order to inhibit the aggressiveness which opposes it, to make it harmless, to get rid of it, perhaps? We have already become acquainted with a few of these methods, but not yet with the one that appears to be the most important. This we can study in the history of the development of the individual. What happens in him to render his desire for aggression innocuous? Something very remarkable, which we should never have guessed and which is nevertheless quite obvious. His aggressiveness is introjected, internalized; it is, in point of fact, sent back to where it came from—that is, it is directed towards his own ego. There it is taken over by a portion of the ego, which sets itself over against the rest of the ego as super-ego, and which now, in the form of 'conscience', is ready to put into action against the ego the same harsh aggressiveness that the ego would have liked to satisfy upon other, extraneous individuals. The tension between the harsh super-ego and the ego that is subjected to it, is called by us the sense of guilt; it expresses itself as a need for punishment. Civilization, therefore, obtains mastery over the individual's dangerous desire for aggression by weakening and disarming it and by setting up an agency within him to watch over it, like a garrison in a conquered city.

As to the origin of the sense of guilt, the analyst has different views from other psychologists; but even he does not find it easy to give an account of it. To begin with, if we ask how a person comes to have a sense of guilt, we arrive at an answer which cannot be disputed: a person feels guilty (devout people would say 'sinful') when he has done something which he knows to be 'bad'. But then we notice how little this answer tells us. Perhaps, after some hesitation, we shall add that even when a person has not actually *done* the bad thing but has only recognized in himself an *intention* to do it, he may regard himself as guilty; and the question then arises of why the intention is regarded as equal to the deed. Both cases, however, presuppose that one had already recognized that what is bad is reprehensible, is something that must not be carried out. How is this judgement arrived at? We may reject the existence of an original, as it were natural, capacity to distinguish good from bad. What is bad is often not at all what is injurious or dangerous to the ego; on the contrary, it may be something which is desirable and enjoyable to the ego. Here, therefore, there is an extraneous influence at work, and it is this that decides what is to be called good or bad. Since a person's own feelings would not have led him along this path, he must have had a motive for submitting to this extraneous influence. Such a motive is easily discovered in his helplessness and his dependence on other people, and it can best be designated as fear of loss of love. If he loses the love of another person upon whom he is dependent, he also ceases to be protected from a variety of dangers. Above all, he is exposed to the danger that this stronger person will show his superiority in the form of punishment. At the beginning, therefore, what is bad is whatever causes one to be threatened with loss of love. For fear of that loss, one must avoid it. This, too, is the reason why it makes little difference whether one has already done the bad thing or only intends to do it. In either case the danger only sets in if and when the authority discovers it, and in either case the authority would behave in the same way.

This state of mind is called a 'bad conscience'; but actually it does not deserve this name, for at this stage the sense of guilt is clearly only a fear of loss of love, 'social' anxiety. In small children it can never be anything else, but in many adults, too, it has only changed to the extent that the place of the father or the two parents is taken by the larger human community. Consequently, such people habitually allow themselves to do any bad thing which promises them enjoyment, so long as they are sure that the authority will not know anything about it or cannot blame them for it; they are afraid only of being found out.[1] Present-day society has to reckon in general with this state of mind.

A great change takes place only when the authority is internalized through the establishment of a super-ego. The phenomena of conscience then reach a higher stage. Actually, it is not until now that we should speak of conscience or a sense of guilt.[2] At this point, too, the fear of being found out comes to

---

[1] This reminds one of Rousseau's famous mandarin.

[2] Everyone of discernment will understand and take into account the fact that in this summary description we have sharply delimited events which in reality occur by gradual transitions, and that it is not merely a question of the *existence* of a super-ego but of its relative strength and sphere of influence. All that has been said above about conscience and guilt is, moreover, common knowledge and almost undisputed.

an end; the distinction, moreover, between doing something bad and wishing to do it disappears entirely, since nothing can be hidden from the super-ego, not even thoughts. It is true that the seriousness of the situation from a real point of view has passed away, for the new authority, the super-ego, has no motive that we know of for ill-treating the ego, with which it is intimately bound up; but genetic influence, which leads to the survival of what is past and has been surmounted, makes itself felt in the fact that fundamentally things remain as they were at the beginning. The super-ego torments the sinful ego with the same feeling of anxiety and is on the watch for opportunities of getting it punished by the external world.

At this second stage of development, the conscience exhibits a peculiarity which was absent from the first stage and which is no longer easy to account for. For the more virtuous a man is, the more severe and distrustful is its behaviour, so that ultimately it is precisely those people who have carried saintliness furthest who reproach themselves with the worst sinfulness. This means that virtue forfeits some part of its promised reward; the docile and continent ego does not enjoy the trust of its mentor, and strives in vain, it would seem, to acquire it. The objection will at once be made that these difficulties are artificial ones, and it will be said that a stricter and more vigilant conscience is precisely the hallmark of a moral man. Moreover, when saints call themselves sinners, they are not so wrong, considering the temptations to instinctual satisfaction to which they are exposed in a specially high degree—since, as is well known, temptations are merely increased by constant frustration, whereas an occasional satisfaction of them causes them to diminish, at least for the time being. The field of ethics, which is so full of problems, presents us with another fact: namely that ill-luck—that is, external frustration—so greatly enhances the power of the conscience in the super-ego. As long as things go well with a man, his conscience is lenient and lets the ego do all sorts of things; but when misfortune befalls him, he searches his soul, acknowledges his sinfulness, heightens the demands of his conscience, imposes abstinences on himself and punishes himself with penances.[3] Whole peoples have behaved in this way, and still do. This, however, is easily explained by the original infantile stage of conscience, which, as we see, is not given up after the introjection into the super-ego, but persists alongside of it and behind it. Fate is regarded as a substitute for the parental agency. If a man is unfortunate it means that he is no longer loved by this highest power; and, threatened by such a loss of love, he once more bows to the parental representative in his super-ego—a representative whom, in his days of good fortune, he was ready to

[3] This enhancing of morality as a consequence of ill-luck has been illustrated by Mark Twain in a delightful little story, *The First Melon I ever Stole*. This first melon happened to be unripe. I heard Mark Twain tell the story himself in one of his public readings. After he had given out the title, he stopped and asked himself as though he was in doubt: '*Was* it the first?' With this, everything had been said. The first melon was evidently not the only one. [This last sentence was added in 1931.—In a letter to Fliess of February 9th, 1898, Freud reported that he had attended a reading by Mark Twain a few days earlier. (Freud, 1950a, Letter 83.)]

neglect. This becomes especially clear where Fate is looked upon in the strictly religious sense of being nothing else than an expression of the Divine Will. The people of Israel had believed themselves to be the favourite child of God, and when the great Father caused misfortune after misfortune to rain down upon this people of his, they were never shaken in their belief in his relationship to them or questioned his power or righteousness. Instead, they produced the prophets, who held up their sinfulness before them; and out of their sense of guilt they created the overstrict commandments of their priestly religion.[4] It is remarkable how differently a primitive man behaves. If he has met with a misfortune, he does not throw the blame on himself but on his fetish, which has obviously not done its duty, and he gives it a thrashing instead of punishing himself.

Thus we know of two origins of the sense of guilt: one arising from fear of an authority, and the other, later on, arising from fear of the super-ego. The first insists upon a renunciation of instinctual satisfactions; the second, as well as doing this, presses for punishment, since the continuance of the forbidden wishes cannot be concealed from the super-ego. We have also learned how the severity of the super-ego—the demands of conscience—is to be understood. It is simply a continuation of

[4] [A very much more extended account of the relations of the people of Israel to their God is to be found in Freud's *Moses and Monotheism* (1939a).]

the severity of the external authority, to which it has succeeded and which it has in part replaced. We now see in what relationship the renunciation of instinct stands to the sense of guilt. Originally, renunciation of instinct was the result of fear of an external authority: one renounced one's satisfactions in order not to lose its love. If one has carried out this renunciation, one is, as it were, quits with the authority and no sense of guilt should remain. But with fear of the super-ego the case is different. Here, instinctual renunciation is not enough, for the wish persists and cannot be concealed from the super-ego. Thus, in spite of the renunciation that has been made, a sense of guilt comes about. This constitutes a great economic disadvantage in the erection of a super-ego, or, as we may put it, in the formation of a conscience. Instinctual renunciation now no longer has a completely liberating effect; virtuous continence is no longer rewarded with the assurance of love. A threatened external unhappiness—loss of love and punishment on the part of the external authority—has been exchanged for a permanent internal unhappiness, for the tension of the sense of guilt.

These interrelations are so complicated and at the same time so important that, at the risk of repeating myself, I shall approach them from yet another angle. The chronological sequence, then, would be as follows. First comes renunciation of instinct owing to fear of aggression by the *external* authority. (This is, of course, what fear of the loss of love amounts to, for love is a protection against this punitive aggression.) After that comes the erection of an *internal* authority, and renunciation of instinct owing to fear of it—owing to fear of conscience. In this second situation bad intentions are equated with bad actions, and hence come a sense of guilt and a need for punishment. The aggressiveness of conscience keeps up the aggressiveness of the authority. So far things have no doubt been made clear; but where does this leave room for the reinforcing influence of misfortune (of renunciation imposed from without), and for the extraordinary severity of conscience in the best and most tractable people? We have already explained both these peculiarities of conscience, but we probably still have an impression that those explanations do not go to the bottom of the matter, and leave a residue still unexplained. And here at last an idea comes in which belongs entirely to psychoanalysis and which is foreign to people's ordinary way of thinking. This idea is of a sort which enables us to understand why the subject-matter was bound to seem so confused and obscure to us. For it tells us that conscience (or more correctly, the anxiety which later becomes conscience) is indeed the cause of instinctual renunciation to begin with, but that later the relationship is reversed. Every renunciation of instinct now becomes a dynamic source of conscience and every fresh renunciation increases the latter's severity and intolerance. If we could only bring it better into harmony with what we already know about the history of the origin of conscience, we should be tempted to defend the paradoxical statement that conscience is the result of instinctual renunciation, or that instinctual renunciation (imposed on us from without) creates conscience, which then demands further instinctual renunciation.

The contradiction between this statement and what we have previously said about the genesis of conscience is in point of fact not so very great, and we see a way of further reducing it. In order to make our exposition easier, let us take as our example the aggressive instinct, and let us assume that the renunciation in question is always a renunciation of aggression. (This, of course, is only to be taken as a temporary assumption.) The effect of instinctual renunciation on the conscience then is that every piece of aggression whose satisfaction the subject gives up is taken over by the super-ego and increases the latter's aggressiveness (against the ego). This does not harmonize well with the view that the original aggressiveness of conscience is a continuance of the severity of the external authority and therefore has nothing to do with renunciation. But the discrepancy is removed if we postulate a different derivation for this first instalment of the super-ego's aggressivity. A considerable amount of aggressiveness must be developed in the child against the authority which prevents him from having his first, but none the less his most important, satisfactions, whatever the kind of instinctual deprivation that is demanded of him may be; but he is obliged to renounce the satisfaction of this revengeful aggressiveness. He finds his way out of this economically difficult situation with the help of familiar mechanisms. By means of identification he takes the unattackable authority into himself. The authority now turns into his super-ego and enters into possession of all the aggressiveness which a child would have liked to exercise against it. The child's ego has to content itself with the unhappy role of the authority—the father—who has been thus degraded. Here, as so often, the [real] situation is reversed: 'If I were the father and you were the child, I should treat you badly.' The relationship between the super-ego and the ego is a return, distorted by a wish, of the real relationships between the ego, as yet undivided, and an external object. That is typical, too. But the essential difference is that the original severity of the super-ego does not—or does not so much—represent the severity which one has experienced from it [the object], or which one attributes to it; it represents rather one's own aggressiveness towards it. If this is correct, we may assert truly that in the beginning conscience arises through the suppression of an aggressive impulse, and that it is subsequently reinforced by fresh suppressions of the same kind.

Which of these two views is correct? The earlier one, which genetically seemed so unassailable, or the newer one, which rounds off the theory in such a welcome fashion? Clearly, and by the evidence, too, of direct observations, both are justified. They do not contradict each other, and they even coincide at one point, for the child's revengeful aggressiveness will be in part determined by the amount of punitive aggression which he expects from his father. Experience shows, however, that the severity of the super-ego which a child develops in no way corresponds to the severity of treatment which he has himself met with.[5] The severity of the former seems to be independent of that of the latter. A child who has been very leniently brought up can acquire a very strict conscience. But it would also be wrong to exaggerate this independence; it is not difficult to convince oneself that severity of upbringing does also exert a strong influence on the formation of the child's super-ego. What it amounts to is that in the formation of the super-ego and the emergence of a conscience innate constitutional factors and influences from the real environment act in combination. This is not at all surprising; on the contrary, it is a universal aetiological condition for all such processes.[6]

It can also be asserted that when a child reacts to his first great instinctual frustrations with excessively strong aggressiveness and with a correspondingly severe super-ego, he is following a phylogenetic model and is going beyond the response that would be currently justified; for the father of

---

[5] As has rightly been emphasized by Melanie Klein and by other, English, writers.

[6] The two main types of pathogenic methods of upbringing—over-strictness and spoiling—have been accurately assessed by Franz Alexander in his book, *The Psychoanalysis of the Total Personality* (1927) in connection with Aichhorn's study of delinquency [*Wayward Youth*, 1925]. The 'unduly lenient and indulgent father' is the cause of children's forming an over-severe super-ego, because, under the impression of the love that they receive, they have no other outlet for their aggressiveness but turning it inwards. In delinquent children, who have been brought up without love, the tension between ego and super-ego is lacking, and the whole of their aggressiveness can be directed outwards. Apart from a constitutional factor which may be supposed to be present, it can be said, therefore, that a severe conscience arises from the joint operation of two factors: the frustration of instinct, which unleashes aggressiveness, and the experience of being loved, which turns the aggressiveness inwards and hands it over to the super-ego.

prehistoric times was undoubtedly terrible, and an extreme amount of aggressiveness may be attributed to him. Thus, if one shifts over from individual to phylogenetic development, the differences between the two theories of the genesis of conscience are still further diminished. On the other hand, a new and important difference makes its appearance between these two developmental processes. We cannot get away from the assumption that man's sense of guilt springs from the Oedipus complex and was acquired at the killing of the father by the brothers banded together.[7] On that occasion an act of aggression was not suppressed but carried out; but it was the same act of aggression whose suppression in the child is supposed to be the source of his sense of guilt. At this point I should not be surprised if the reader were to exclaim angrily: 'So it makes no difference whether one kills one's father or not—one gets a feeling of guilt in either case! We may take leave to raise a few doubts here. Either it is not true that the sense of guilt comes from suppressed aggressiveness, or else the whole story of the killing of the father is a fiction and the children of primaeval man did not kill their fathers any more often than children do nowadays. Besides, if it is not fiction but a plausible piece of history, it would be a case of something happening which everyone expects to happen—namely, of a person feeling guilty because he really has done something which cannot be justi-

[7] [*Totem and Taboo* (1912–13).]

fied. And of this event, which is after all an everyday occur-rence, psycho-analysis has not yet given any explanation.'

That is true, and we must make good the omission. Nor is there any great secret about the matter. When one has a sense of guilt after having committed a misdeed, and because of it, the feeling should more properly be called *remorse*. It relates only to a deed that has been done, and, of course, it presup-poses that a *conscience*—the readiness to feel guilty—was already in existence before the deed took place. Remorse of this sort can, therefore, never help us to discover the origin of conscience and of the sense of guilt in general. What happens in these everyday cases is usually this: an instinctual need acquires the strength to achieve satisfaction in spite of the con-science, which is, after all, limited in its strength; and with the natural weakening of the need owing to its having been satis-fied, the former balance of power is restored. Psycho-analysis is thus justified in excluding from the present discussion the case of a sense of guilt due to remorse, however frequently such cases occur and however great their practical importance.

But if the human sense of guilt goes back to the killing of the primal father, that was after all a case of 'remorse'. Are we to assume that [at that time] a conscience and a sense of guilt were not, as we have presupposed, in existence before the deed? If not, where, in this case, did the remorse come from? There is no doubt that this case should explain the secret of the sense of guilt to us and put an end to our difficulties. And I believe it does. This remorse was the result of the primordial ambivalence of feeling towards the father. His sons hated him, but they loved him, too. After their hatred had been satisfied by their act of aggression, their love came to the fore in their remorse for the deed. It set up the super-ego by identification with the father; it gave that agency the father's power, as though as a punishment for the deed of aggression they had carried out against him, and it created the restrictions which were intended to prevent a repetition of the deed. And since the inclination to aggressiveness against the father was repeated in the following generations, the sense of guilt, too, persisted, and it was reinforced once more by every piece of aggressiveness that was suppressed and carried over to the super-ego. Now, I think, we can at last grasp two things perfectly clearly: the part played by love in the origin of conscience and the fatal inevitability of the sense of guilt. Whether one has killed one's father or has abstained from doing so is not really the decisive thing. One is bound to feel guilty in either case, for the sense of guilt is an expression of the conflict due to ambivalence, of the external struggle between Eros and the instinct of destruction or death. This conflict is set going as soon as men are faced with the task of living together. So long as the community assumes no other form than that of the family, the conflict is bound to express itself in the Oedipus complex, to establish the conscience and to create the first sense of guilt. When an attempt is made to widen the community, the same conflict is continued in forms which are dependent on the past; and it is strengthened and results in a further intensification of the sense of guilt. Since civilization obeys an internal erotic impulsion which causes human beings to unite in a closely-knit group, it can only achieve this aim through an ever-increasing reinforcement of the sense of guilt. What began in relation to the father is completed in relation to the group. If civilization is a necessary course of development from the family to humanity as a whole, then—as a result of the inborn conflict arising from ambivalence, of the eternal struggle between the trends of love and death—there is inextricably bound up with it an increase of the sense of guilt, which will perhaps reach heights that the individual finds hard to tolerate. One is reminded of the great poet's moving arraignment of the 'Heavenly Powers':—

> *Ihr führt in's Leben uns hinein.*
> *Ihr lasst den Armen schuldig werden,*
> *Dann überlasst Ihr ihn den Pein,*
> *Denn jede Schuld rächt sich auf Erden.*[8]

[8] One of the Harp-player's songs in Goethe's *Wilhelm Meister*.

> [To earth, this weary earth, ye bring us
> To guilt ye let us heedless go,
> Then leave repentance fierce to wring us:
> A moment's guilt, an age of woe!
>   Carlyle's translation.

The first couplet appears as an association to a dream in Freud's short book *On Dreams* (1901a), *Standard Ed.*, 5, 637 and 639.]

And we may well heave a sigh of relief at the thought that it is nevertheless vouchsafed to a few to salvage without effort from the whirlpool of their own feelings the deepest truths, towards which the rest of us have to find our way through tormenting uncertainty and with restless groping.

VIII

Having reached the end of his journey, the author must ask his readers' forgiveness for not having been a more skilful guide and for not having spared them empty stretches of road and troublesome *détours*. There is no doubt that it could have been done better. I will attempt, late in the day, to make some amends.

In the first place, I suspect that the reader has the impression that our discussions on the sense of guilt disrupt the framework of this essay: that they take up too much space, so that the rest of its subject-matter, with which they are not always closely connected, is pushed to one side. This may have spoilt the structure of my paper; but it corresponds faithfully to my intention to represent the sense of guilt as the most important problem in the development of civilization and to show that the price we pay for our advance in civilization is a loss of hap-

piness through the heightening of the sense of guilt.[1] Anything
that still sounds strange about this statement, which is the final
conclusion of our investigation, can probably be traced to the
quite peculiar relationship—as yet completely unexplained—
which the sense of guilt has to our consciousness. In the common case of remorse, which we regard as normal, this feeling
makes itself clearly enough perceptible to consciousness.
Indeed, we are accustomed to speak of a 'consciousness of guilt'
instead of a 'sense of guilt'.[2] Our study of the neuroses, to
which, after all, we owe the most valuable pointers to an
understanding of normal conditions, brings us up against some
contradictions. In one of those affections, obsessional neurosis,
the sense of guilt makes itself noisily heard in consciousness; it

[1] 'Thus conscience does make cowards of us all . . . '
That the education of young people at the present day conceals from them the
part which sexuality will play in their lives is not the only reproach which we are
obliged to make against it. Its other sin is that it does not prepare them for the
aggressiveness of which they are destined to become the objects. In sending the
young out into life with such a false psychological orientation, education is behav-
ing as though one were to equip people starting on a Polar expedition with summer
clothing and maps of the Italian Lakes. In this it becomes evident that a certain mis-
use is being made of ethical demands. The strictness of those demands would not
do so much harm if education were to say: 'This is how men ought to be, in order
to be happy and to make others happy; but you have to reckon on their not being
like that.' Instead of this the young are made to believe that everyone else fulfills
those ethical demands—that is, that everyone else is virtuous. It is on this that the
demand is based that the young, too, shall become virtuous.
[2] ['Schuldbewusstsein' instead of 'Schuldgefühl'. The second of these terms is the one
which Freud has been using for the most part. They are synonyms apart from their
literal meaning, and both are translated by the usual English 'sense of guilt' except
on such special occasions as this.]

dominates the clinical picture and the patient's life as well, and it hardly allows anything else to appear alongside of it. But in most other cases and forms of neurosis it remains completely unconscious, without on that account producing any less important effects. Our patients do not believe us when we attribute an 'unconscious sense of guilt' to them. In order to make ourselves at all intelligible to them, we tell them of an unconscious need for punishment, in which the sense of guilt finds expression. But its connection with a particular form of neurosis must not be over-estimated. Even in obsessional neurosis there are types of patients who are not aware of their sense of guilt, or who only feel it as a tormenting uneasiness, a kind of anxiety, if they are prevented from carrying out certain actions. It ought to be possible eventually to understand these things; but as yet we cannot. Here perhaps we may be glad to have it pointed out that the sense of guilt is at bottom nothing else but a topographical variety of anxiety; in its later phases it coincides completely with *fear of the super-ego*. And the relations of anxiety to consciousness exhibit the same extraordinary variations. Anxiety is always present somewhere or other behind every symptom; but at one time it takes noisy possession of the whole of consciousness, while at another it conceals itself so completely that we are obliged to speak of unconscious anxiety or, if we want to have a clearer psychological conscience, since anxiety is in the first instance simply a feeling, of possibilities of anxiety. Consequently it is very conceivable that the sense of guilt produced by civilization is not

perceived as such either, and remains to a large extent unconscious, or appears as a sort of *malaise*,[3] a dissatisfaction, for
which people seek other motivations. Religions, at any rate,
have never overlooked the part played in civilization by a
sense of guilt. Furthermore—a point which I failed to appreciate elsewhere[4]—they claim to redeem mankind from this sense
of guilt, which they call sin. From the manner in which, in
Christianity, this redemption is achieved—by the sacrificial
death of a single person, who in this manner takes upon himself a guilt that is common to everyone—we have been able to
infer what the first occasion may have been on which this primal guilt, which was also the beginning of civilization, was
acquired.[5]

Though it cannot be of great importance, it may not be
superfluous to elucidate the meaning of a few words such as
'super-ego', 'conscience', 'sense of guilt', 'need for punishment'
and 'remorse', which we have often, perhaps, used too loosely
and interchangeably. They all relate to the same state of affairs,
but denote different aspects of it. The super-ego is an agency
which has been inferred by us, and conscience is a function
which we ascribe, among other functions, to that agency. This
function consists in keeping a watch over the actions and
intentions of the ego and judging them, in exercising a censor-
ship. The sense of guilt, the harshness of the super-ego, is thus

---

[3] ['*Unbehagen*': the word which appears in the title of this work.]
[4] In *The Future of an Illusion* (1927c).
[5] *Totem and Taboo* (1912–13).

the same thing as the severity of the conscience. It is the perception which the ego has of being watched over in this way, the assessment of the tension between its own strivings and the demands of the super-ego. The fear of this critical agency (a fear which is at the bottom of the whole relationship), the need for punishment, is an instinctual manifestation on the part of the ego, which has become masochistic under the influence of a sadistic super-ego; it is a portion, that is to say, of the instinct towards internal destruction present in the ego, employed for forming an erotic attachment to the super-ego. We ought not to speak of a conscience until a super-ego is demonstrably present. As to a sense of guilt, we must admit that it is in existence before the super-ego, and therefore before conscience, too. At that time it is the immediate expression of fear of the external authority, a recognition of the tension between the ego and that authority. It is the direct derivative of the conflict between the need for the authority's love and the urge towards instinctual satisfaction, whose inhibition produces the inclination to aggression. The superimposition of these two strata of the sense of guilt—one coming from fear of the *external* authority, the other from fear of the *internal* authority—has hampered our insight into the position of conscience in a number of ways. Remorse is a general term for the ego's reaction in a case of sense of guilt. It contains, in little altered form, the sensory material of the anxiety which is operating behind the sense of guilt; it is itself a punishment and can include the need for punishment. Thus remorse, too, can be older than conscience.

Nor will it do any harm if we once more review the contradictions which have for a while perplexed us during our
enquiry. Thus, at one point the sense of guilt was the consequence of acts of aggression that had been abstained from; but
at another point—and precisely at its historical beginning, the
killing of the father—it was the consequence of an act of
aggression that had been carried out. But a way out of this difficulty was found. For the institution of the internal authority,
the super-ego, altered the situation radically. Before this, the
sense of guilt coincided with remorse. (We may remark, inci-
dentally, that the term 'remorse' should be reserved for the
reaction after an act of aggression has actually been carried
out.) After this, owing to the omniscience of the super-ego, the
difference between an aggression intended and an aggression
carried out lost its force. Henceforward a sense of guilt could
be produced not only by an act of violence that is actually carried out (as all the world knows), but also by one that is merely
intended (as psycho-analysis has discovered). Irrespectively of
this alteration in the psychological situation, the conflict arising from ambivalence—the conflict between the two primal
instincts—leaves the same result behind. We are tempted to
look here for the solution of the problem of the varying relation in which the sense of guilt stands to consciousness. It
might be thought that a sense of guilt arising from remorse for
an evil *deed* must always be conscious, whereas a sense of guilt
arising from the perception of an evil *impulse* may remain

unconscious. But the answer is not so simple as that. Obsessional neurosis speaks energetically against it.

The second contradiction concerned the aggressive energy with which we suppose the super-ego to be endowed. According to one view, that energy merely carries on the punitive energy of the external authority and keeps it alive in the mind [p. 121]; while, according to another view, it consists, on the contrary, of one's own aggressive energy which has not been used and which one now directs against that inhibiting authority [p. 128]. The first view seemed to fit in better with the *history*, and the second with the *theory*, of the sense of guilt. Closer reflection has resolved this apparently irreconcilable contradiction almost too completely; what remained as the essential and common factor was that in each case we were dealing with an aggressiveness which had been displaced inwards. Clinical observation, moreover, allows us in fact to distinguish two sources for the aggressiveness which we attribute to the super-ego; one or the other of them exercises the stronger effect in any given case, but as a general rule they operate in unison.

This is, I think, the place at which to put forward for serious consideration a view which I have earlier recommended for provisional acceptance.[6] In the most recent analytic literature a predilection is shown for the idea that any kind of frustration, any thwarted instinctual satisfaction, results, or may result, in a

---

[6] [It has not been possible to trace this earlier recommendation.]

heightening of the sense of guilt.[7] A great theoretical simplification will, I think, be achieved if we regard this as applying
only to the *aggressive* instincts, and little will be found to contradict this assumption. For how are we to account, on dynamic
and economic grounds, for an increase in the sense of guilt
appearing in place of an unfulfilled *erotic* demand? This only
seems possible in a round-about way—if we suppose, that is,
that the prevention of an erotic satisfaction calls up a piece
of aggressiveness against the person who has interfered with
the satisfaction, and that this aggressiveness has itself to be
suppressed in turn. But if this is so, it is after all only the aggressiveness which is transformed into a sense of guilt, by being
suppressed and made over to the super-ego. I am convinced
that many processes will admit of a simpler and clearer exposition
if the findings of psycho-analysis with regard to the derivation of
the sense of guilt are restricted to the aggressive instincts.
Examination of the clinical material gives us no unequivocal
answer here, because, as our hypothesis tells us, the two classes
of instinct hardly ever appear in a pure form, isolated from
each other; but an investigation of extreme cases would probably point in the direction I anticipate.

I am tempted to extract a first advantage from this more
restricted view of the case by applying it to the process of
repression. As we have learned, neurotic symptoms are, in their

[7] This view is taken in particular by Ernest Jones, Susan Isaacs and Melanie Klein;
and also, I understand, by Reik and Alexander.

essence, substitutive satisfactions for unfulfilled sexual wishes. In the course of our analytic work we have discovered to our surprise that perhaps every neurosis conceals a quota of uncon- scious sense of guilt, which in its turn fortifies the symptoms by making use of them as a punishment. It now seems plausi- ble to formulate the following proposition. When an instinc- tual trend undergoes repression, its libidinal elements are turned into symptoms, and its aggressive components into a sense of guilt. Even if this proposition is only an average approximation to the truth, it is worthy of our interest.

Some readers of this work may further have an impression that they have heard the formula of the struggle between Eros and the death instinct too often. It was alleged to characterize the process of civilization which mankind undergoes [p. 118] but it was also brought into connection with the development of the individual [p. 112], and, in addition, it was said to have revealed the secret of organic life in general [p. 113f]. We can- not, I think, avoid going into the relations of these three processes to one another. The repetition of the same formula is justified by the consideration that both the process of human civilization and of the development of the individual are also vital processes—which is to say that they must share in the most general characteristic of life. On the other hand, evi- dence of the presence of this general characteristic fails, for the very reason of its general nature, to help us to arrive at any dif- ferentiation [between the processes], so long as it is not nar- rowed down by special qualifications. We can only be satisfied, therefore, if we assert that the process of civilization is a modification which the vital process experiences under the influence of a task that is set it by Eros and instigated by Ananke—by the exigencies of reality; and that this task is one of uniting separate individuals into a community bound together by libidinal ties. When, however, we look at the relation between the process of human civilization and the developmental or educative process of individual human beings, we shall conclude without much hesitation that the two are very similar in nature, if not the very same process applied to different kinds of object. The process of the civilization of the human species is, of course, an abstraction of a higher order than is the development of the individual and it is therefore harder to apprehend in concrete terms, nor should we pursue analogies to an obsessional extreme; but in view of the similarity between the aims of the two processes—in the one case the integration of a separate individual into a human group, and in the other case the creation of a unified group out of many individuals—we cannot be surprised at the similarity between the means employed and the resultant phenomena.

In view of its exceptional importance, we must not long postpone the mention of one feature which distinguishes between the two processes. In the developmental process of the individual, the programme of the pleasure principle, which consists in finding the satisfaction of happiness, is retained as the main aim. Integration in, or adaptation to, a human community appears as a scarcely avoidable condition which must be fulfilled before this aim of happiness can be achieved. If it could be done without that condition, it would perhaps be preferable. To put it in other words, the development of the individual seems to us to be a product of the interaction between two urges, the urge towards happiness, which we usually call 'egoistic', and the urge towards union with others in the community, which we call 'altruistic'. Neither of these descriptions goes much below the surface. In the process of individual development, as we have said, the main accent falls mostly on the egoistic urge (or the urge towards happiness), while the other urge, which may be described as a 'cultural' one, is usually content with the role of imposing restrictions. But in the process of civilization things are different. Here by far the most important thing is the aim of creating a unity out of the individual human beings. It is true that the aim of happiness is still there, but it is pushed into the background. It almost seems as if the creation of a great human community would be most successful if no attention had to be paid to the happiness of the individual. The developmental process of the individual can thus be expected to have special features of its own which are not reproduced in the process of human civilization. It is only in so far as the first of these processes has union with the community as its aim that it need coincide with the second process.

Just as a planet revolves around a central body as well as rotating on its own axis, so the human individual takes part in the course of development of mankind at the same time as he pursues his own path in life. But to our dull eyes the play of forces in the heavens seems fixed in a never-changing order; in the field of organic life we can still see how the forces contend with one another, and how the effects of the conflict are continually changing. So, also, the two urges, the one towards personal happiness and the other towards union with other human beings must struggle with each other in every individual; and so, also, the two processes of individual and of cultural development must stand in hostile opposition to each other and mutually dispute the ground. But this struggle between the individual and society is not a derivative of the contradiction— probably an irreconcilable one—between the primal instincts of Eros and death. It is a dispute within the economics of the libido, comparable to the contest concerning the distribution of libido between ego and objects; and it does admit of an eventual accommodation in the individual, as, it may be hoped, it will also do in the future of civilization, however much that civilization may oppress the life of the individual to-day.

The analogy between the process of civilization and the path of individual development may be extended in an important respect. It can be asserted that the community, too, evolves a super-ego under whose influence cultural development proceeds. It would be a tempting task for anyone who has a knowledge of human civilizations to follow out this analogy in detail. I will confine myself to bringing forward a few striking points. The super-ego of an epoch of civilization has an origin similar to that of an individual. It is based on the impression left behind by the personalities of great leaders—men of overwhelming force of mind or men in whom one of the human impulsions has found its strongest and purest, and therefore often its most one-sided, expression In many instances the analogy goes still further, in that during their lifetime these figures were—often enough, even if not always—mocked and maltreated by others and even despatched in a cruel fashion.\In the same way, indeed, the primal father did not attain divinity until long after he had met his death by violence. The most arresting example of this fateful conjunction is to be seen in the figure of Jesus Christ—if, indeed, that figure is not a part of mythology, which called it into being from an obscure memory of that primal event. Another point of agreement between the cultural and the individual super-ego is that the former, just like the latter, sets up strict ideal demands, disobedience to which is visited with 'fear of conscience' [p. 128]. Here, indeed, we come across the remarkable circumstance that the mental processes concerned are actually more familiar to us and more accessible to consciousness as they are seen in the group than they can be in the individual man. In him, when tension arises, it is only the aggressiveness of the super-ego which, in the form of reproaches, makes itself noisily heard; its actual demands often remain unconscious in the background. If we bring them to conscious knowledge, we find that they coincide with the precepts of the prevailing cultural super-ego. At this point the two processes, that of the cultural development of the group and that of the cultural development of the individual, are, as it were, always interlocked. For that reason some of the manifestations and properties of the super-ego can be more easily detected in its behaviour in the cultural community than in the separate individual.

The cultural super-ego has developed its ideals and set up its demands. Among the latter, those which deal with the relations of human beings to one another are comprised under the heading of ethics. People have at all times set the greatest value on ethics, as though they expected that it in particular would produce especially important results. And it does in fact deal with a subject which can easily be recognized as the sorest spot in every civilization. Ethics is thus to be regarded as a therapeutic attempt—as an endeavour to achieve, by means of a command of the super-ego, something which has so far not been achieved by means of any other cultural activities. As we already know, the problem before us is how to get rid of the greatest hindrance to civilization—namely, the constitutional inclination of human beings to be aggressive towards one another; and for that very reason we are especially interested in what is probably the most recent of the cultural commands of the super-ego, the commandment to love one's neighbour as oneself. In our research into, and therapy of, a neurosis, we are led to make two reproaches against the super-ego of the individual. In the severity of its commands and prohibitions it troubles itself too little about the happiness of the ego, in that it takes insufficient account of the resistances against obeying them—of the instinctual strength of the id [in the first place],

and of the difficulties presented by the real external environment [in the second]. Consequently we are very often obliged,
for therapeutic purposes, to oppose the super-ego, and we
endeavour to lower its demands. Exactly the same objections
can be made against the ethical demands of the cultural super-
ego. It, too, does not trouble itself enough about the facts of
the mental constitution of human beings. It issues a command
and does not ask whether it is possible for people to obey it.
On the contrary, it assumes that a man's ego is psychologically
capable of anything that is required of it, that his ego has
unlimited mastery over his id. This is a mistake; and even in
what are known as normal people the id cannot be controlled
beyond certain limits. If more is demanded of a man, a revolt
will be produced in him or a neurosis, or he will be made
unhappy. The commandment, 'Love thy neighbour as thyself',
is the strongest defence against human aggressiveness and an
excellent example of the unpsychological proceedings of the
cultural super-ego. The commandment is impossible to fulfil;
such an enormous inflation of love can only lower its value, not
get rid of the difficulty. Civilization pays no attention to all
this; it merely admonishes us that the harder it is to obey the
precept the more meritorious it is to do so. But anyone who
follows such a precept in present-day civilization only puts
himself at a disadvantage *vis-à-vis* the person who disregards it.
What a potent obstacle to civilization aggressiveness must be,
if the defence against it can cause as much unhappiness as
aggressiveness itself! 'Natural' ethics, as it is called, has nothing

to offer here except the narcissistic satisfaction of being able to think oneself better than others. At this point the ethics based on religion introduces its promises of a better afterlife. But so long as virtue is not rewarded here on earth, ethics will, I fancy, preach in vain. I too think it quite certain that a real change in the relations of human beings to possessions would be of more help in this direction than any ethical commands; but the recognition of this fact among socialists has been obscured and made useless for practical purposes by a fresh idealistic misconception of human nature. [Cf. p. 106 above.]

I believe the line of thought which seeks to trace in the phenomena of cultural development the part played by a super-ego promises still further discoveries. I hasten to come to a close. But there is one question which I can hardly evade. If the development of civilization has such a far-reaching similarity to the development of the individual and if it employs the same methods, may we not be justified in reaching the diagnosis that, under the influence of cultural urges, some civilizations, or some epochs of civilization—possibly the whole of mankind—have become 'neurotic'?[8] An analytic dissection of such neuroses might lead to therapeutic recommendations which could lay claim to great practical interest. I would not say that an attempt of this kind to carry psycho-analysis over to the cultural community was absurd or doomed to be fruitless. But we should have to be very cautious and not forget

---

[8] Cf. some remarks in *The Future of an Illusion* (1927c).

that, after all, we are only dealing with analogies and that it is dangerous, not only with men but also with concepts, to tear them from the sphere in which they have originated and been evolved. Moreover, the diagnosis of communal neuroses is faced with a special difficulty. In an individual neurosis we take as our starting-point the contrast that distinguishes the patient from his environment, which is assumed to be 'normal'. For a group all of whose members are affected by one and the same disorder no such background could exist; it would have to be found elsewhere. And as regards the therapeutic application of our knowledge, what would be the use of the most correct analysis of social neuroses, since no one possesses authority to impose such a therapy upon the group? But in spite of all these difficulties, we may expect that one day someone will venture to embark upon a pathology of cultural communities.

For a wide variety of reasons, it is very far from my intention to express an opinion upon the value of human civilization. I have endeavoured to guard myself against the enthusiastic prejudice which holds that our civilization is the most precious thing that we possess or could acquire and that its path will necessarily lead to heights of unimagined perfection. I can at least listen without indignation to the critic who is of the opinion that when one surveys the aims of cultural endeavour and the means it employs, one is bound to come to the conclusion that the whole effort is not worth the trouble, and that the outcome of it can only be a state of affairs which the individual

will be unable to tolerate. My impartiality is made all the easier to me by my knowing very little about all these things. One
thing only do I know for certain and that is that man's judgements of value follow directly his wishes for happiness—that,
accordingly, they are an attempt to support his illusions with
arguments. I should find it very understandable if someone
were to point out the obligatory nature of the course of human
civilization and were to say, for instance, that the tendencies to
a restriction of sexual life or to the institution of a humanitar-
ian ideal at the expense of natural selection were developmental trends which cannot be averted or turned aside and to
which it is best for us to yield as though they were necessities
of nature. I know, too, the objection that can be made against
this, to the effect that in the history of mankind, trends such as
these, which were considered unsurmountable, have often
been thrown aside and replaced by other trends. Thus I have
not the courage to rise up before my fellow-men as a prophet,
and I bow to their reproach that I can offer them no consolation: for at bottom that is what they are all demanding—the
wildest revolutionaries no less passionately than the most virtuous believers.

The fateful question for the human species seems to me to
be whether and to what extent their cultural development will
succeed in mastering the disturbance of their communal life by
the human instinct of aggression and self-destruction. It may
be that in this respect precisely the present time deserves a special interest. Men have gained control over the forces of nature

to such an extent that with their help they would have no difficulty in exterminating one another to the last man. They know this, and hence comes a large part of their current unrest, their unhappiness and their mood of anxiety. And now it is to be expected that the other of the two 'Heavenly Powers' [p. 135], eternal Eros, will make an effort to assert himself in the struggle with his equally immortal adversary. But who can foresee with what success and with what result?[9]

[9][The final sentence was added in 1931—when the menace of Hitler was already beginning to be apparent.]

SIGMUND FREUD: A BRIEF LIFE

by Peter Gay

I T WAS FREUD'S fate, as he observed not without pride, to "agitate the sleep of mankind." Half a century after his death, it seems clear that he succeeded far better than he expected, though in ways he would not have appreciated. It is commonplace but true that we all speak Freud now, correctly or not. We casually refer to oedipal conflicts and sibling rivalry, narcissism and Freudian slips. But before we can speak that way with authority, we must read his writings attentively. They repay reading, with dividends.

Sigmund Freud was born on May 6, 1856, in the small Moravian town of Freiberg.[1] His father, Jacob Freud, was an impecunious merchant; his mother, Amalia, was handsome,

---

[1] His given names were Sigismund Schlomo, but he never used his middle name and, after experimenting with the shorter form for some time, definitively adopted the first name Sigmund—on occasion relapsing into the original formulation—in the early 1870s, when he was a medical student at the University of Vienna. Freiberg, now in Czechoslovakia, bears the Czech name "Pribor."

self-assertive, and young—twenty years her husband's junior and his third wife. Jacob Freud had two sons from his first marriage who were about Amalia Freud's age and lived nearby. One of these half brothers had a son, John, who, though Sigmund Freud's nephew, was older than his uncle. Freud's family constellation, then, was intricate enough to puzzle the clever and inquisitive youngster. Inquisitiveness, the natural endowment of children, was particularly marked in him. Life would provide ample opportunity to satisfy it.

In 1860, when Freud was almost four, he moved with his family to Vienna, then a magnet for many immigrants. This was the opening phase of the Hapsburg Empire's liberal era. Jews, only recently freed from onerous taxes and humiliating restrictions on their property rights, professional choices, and religious practices, could realistically harbor hopes for economic advancement, political participation, and a measure of social acceptance. This was the time, Freud recalled, when "every industrious Jewish school boy carried a Cabinet Minister's portfolio in his satchel."[2] The young Freud was encouraged to cultivate high ambitions. As his mother's first-born and a family favorite, he secured, once his family could afford it, a room of his own. He showed marked gifts from his first school days, and in his secondary school, or Gymnasium, he was first in his class year after year.

In 1873, at seventeen, Freud entered the University of

[2] *The Interpretation of Dreams* (1900), *SE* IV, 193.

Vienna. He had planned to study law, but, driven on by what he called his "greed for knowledge," instead matriculated in the faculty of medicine, intending to embark, not on a conventional career as a physician, but on philosophical-scientific investigations that might solve some of the great riddles that fascinated him. He found his work in physiology and neurology so absorbing that he did not take his degree until 1881.

A brilliant researcher, he cultivated the habit of close observation and the congenial stance of scientific skepticism. He was privileged to work under professors with international reputations, almost all German imports and tough-minded positivists who disdained metaphysical speculations about, let alone pious explanations of, natural phenomena. Even after Freud modified their theories of the mind—in essence barely disguised physiological theories—he recalled his teachers with unfeigned gratitude. The most memorable of them, Ernst Brücke, an illustrious physiologist and a civilized but exacting taskmaster, confirmed Freud's bent as an unbeliever. Freud had grown up with no religious instruction at home, came to Vienna University as an atheist, and left it as an atheist—with persuasive scientific arguments.

In 1882, on Brücke's advice, Freud reluctantly left the laboratory to take a lowly post at the Vienna General Hospital. The reason was romantic: in April, he had met Martha Bernays, a slender, attractive young woman from northern Germany visiting one of his sisters, and fallen passionately in love. He was soon secretly engaged to her, but too poor to establish the respectable bourgeois household that he and his fiancée thought essential. It was not until September 1886, some five months after opening his practice in Vienna, with the aid of wedding gifts and loans from affluent friends, that the couple could marry. Within nine years, they had six children, the last of whom, Anna, grew up to be her father's confidante, secretary, nurse, disciple, and representative, and an eminent psychoanalyst in her own right.

Before his marriage, from October 1885 to February 1886, Freud worked in Paris with the celebrated French neurologist Jean-Martin Charcot, who impressed Freud with his bold advocacy of hypnosis as an instrument for healing medical disorders, and no less bold championship of the thesis (then quite unfashionable) that hysteria is an ailment to which men are susceptible no less than women.\ Charcot, an unrivaled observer, stimulated Freud's growing interest in the theoretical and therapeutic aspects of mental healing. Nervous ailments became Freud's specialty, and in the 1890s, as he told a friend, psychology became his tyrant. During these years he founded the psychoanalytic theory of mind.

He had intriguing if somewhat peculiar help. In 1887, he had met a nose-and-throat specialist from Berlin, Wilhelm Fliess, and rapidly established an intimate friendship with him. Fliess was the listener the lonely Freud craved: an intellectual gambler shocked at no idea, a propagator of provocative (at times fruitful) theories, an enthusiast who fed Freud ideas on which he could build. For over a decade, Fliess and Freud exchanged confidential letters and technical memoranda, meeting occasionally to explore their subversive notions. And Freud was propelled toward the discovery of psychoanalysis in his practice: his patients proved excellent teachers. He was increasingly specializing in women suffering from hysteria, and, observing their symptoms and listening to their complaints, he found that, though a good listener, he did not listen carefully enough. They had much to tell him.

In 1895, Freud and his fatherly friend Josef Breuer, a thriving, generous internist, published *Studies on Hysteria*, assigning Breuer's former patient "Anna O." pride of place. She had furnished fascinating material for intimate conversations between Breuer and Freud, and was to become, quite against her—and Breuer's—will, the founding patient of psychoanalysis. She demonstrated to Freud's satisfaction that hysteria originates in sexual malfunctioning and that symptoms can be talked away.

The year 1895 was decisive for Freud in other ways. In July, Freud managed to analyze a dream, his own, fully. He would employ this dream, known as "Irma's injection," as a model for psychoanalytic dream interpretation when he published it, some four years later, in his *Interpretation of Dreams*. In the fall, he drafted, but neither completed nor published, what was later called the Project for a Scientific Psychology. It anticipated some of his fundamental theories yet serves as a reminder that Freud had been deeply enmeshed in the traditional physiological interpretation of mental events.

Increasingly Freud was offering psychological explanations

for psychological phenomena. In the spring of 1896, he first used the fateful name, "psychoanalysis." Then in October his father died; "the most important event," he recalled a dozen years later, "the most poignant loss, of a man's life."[3] It supplied a powerful impetus toward psychoanalytic theorizing, stirring Freud to his unprecedented self-analysis, more systematic and thoroughgoing than the frankest autobiographer's self-probing. In the next three or four years, as he labored over his "Dream book," new discoveries crowded his days. But first he had to jettison the "seduction theory" he had championed for some time. It held that *every* neurosis results from premature sexual activity, mainly child molestation, in childhood.[4] Once freed from this far-reaching but improbable theory, Freud could appreciate the share of fantasies in mental life, and discover the Oedipus complex, that universal family triangle.

Freud's *Interpretation of Dreams* was published in November 1899.[5] It treated all dreams as wish fulfillments, detailed the mental stratagems that translate their causes into the strange drama the awakening dreamer remembers, and, in the difficult seventh chapter, outlined a comprehensive theory of mind. Its first reception was cool. During six years, only 351 copies were

---

[3] Ibid., xxvi.

[4] Freud never claimed that sexual abuse does not exist. He had patients who he knew had not imagined the assaults they reported. All he abandoned when he abandoned the seduction theory was the sweeping claim that *only* the rape of a child, whether a boy or a girl, by a servant, an older sibling, or a classmate, could be the cause of a neurosis.

[5] The book bears the date of 1900 on the title page and this date is usually given as the date of publication.

sold, a second edition did not appear until 1909. However, Freud's popularly written *Psychopathology of Everyday Life* of 1901 found a wider audience. Its collection of appealing slips of all sorts made Freud's fundamental point that the mind, however disheveled it might appear, is governed by firm rules. Thus— to give but one typical instance—the presiding officer of the Austrian parliament, facing a disagreeable season, opened it with the formal declaration that it was hereby closed. That "accident" had been prompted by his hidden repugnance for the sessions ahead.

Gradually, though still considered a radical, Freud acquired prestige and supporters. He had quarreled with Fliess in 1900, and, though their correspondence lingered on for some time, the two men never met again. Yet in 1902, after unconscionable delays, apparently generated by anti-Semitism combined with distrust of the maverick innovator, he was finally appointed an associate professor at the University of Vienna. Late that year, Freud and four other Viennese physicians began meeting every Wednesday night in his apartment at Berggasse 19 to discuss psychoanalytic questions; four years after, the group, grown to over a dozen regular participants, employed a paid secretary (Otto Rank) to take minutes and keep records. Finally, in 1908, it was transformed into the Vienna Psychoanalytic Society. At least some medical men (and a few women) were taking Freud's ideas seriously.

In 1905, Freud buttressed the structure of psychoanalytic thought with the second pillar of his theory: the *Three Essays on the Theory of Sexuality*. It outlined perversions and "normal" development from childhood to puberty with a lack of censoriousness and an openness hitherto virtually unknown in medical literature. Again in 1905, Freud brought out his book on jokes and the first of his famous case histories: "Fragment of an Analysis of a Case of Hysteria," nicknamed the "Dora case." He published it to illustrate the uses of dream interpretation in psychoanalysis, and expose his failure to recognize the power of transference in the analytic situation, but its lack of empathy with his embattled teen-age analysand has made it controversial.

In the following decade, Freud enriched the technique of psychoanalysis with three more sophisticated case histories—"Analysis of a Phobia in a Five-Year-Old Boy" ("Little Hans"), "Notes upon a Case of Obsessional Neurosis" ("Rat Man") in 1909, and "Psycho-Analytic Notes on an Autobiographical Account of a Case of Paranoia" ("Schreber Case") in 1911. Despite recent reanalyses, they remain lucid expository models across a wide spectrum of mental ailments. Then, from 1910 on, Freud published pioneering, exceedingly influential papers on technique, to establish psychoanalytic method on sound foundations. Nor did he neglect theory; witness such an important paper as "Formulations on the Two Principles of Mental Functioning" (1911), in which he differentiated between the "primary process," the primitive, unconscious element in the mind, and the "secondary process," largely conscious and controlled.

During these years, Freud also broke out of the circumscribed bounds of clinical and theoretical specialization by publishing papers on religion, literature, sexual mores, biography, sculpture, prehistory, and much else. "Obsessive Actions and Religious Practices" (1907), "Creative Writers and Daydreaming" (1908), "'Civilized' Sexual Morality and Modern Nervous Illness" (1908), and his widely debated study of the origins of homosexuality, "Leonardo da Vinci and a Memory of His Childhood" (1910), are only samples of his range. Freud took all of culture as his province. He was realizing the program he had outlined for himself in his youth to solve some of the great riddles of human existence.

Yet Freud also found the decade from 1905 to 1914 agitating with the progress of, and disagreeable splits within, a rapidly emerging international movement—his movement. Psychoanalytic politics took center stage. Two principal sources of hope for the future of Freud's ideas, and later of envenomed contention, were the intelligent, Socialist Viennese physician Alfred Adler (1870–1937), and the original, self-willed Swiss psychiatrist Carl G. Jung (1875–1961). Adler had been among Freud's earliest adherents and remained for some years his most prominent Viennese advocate. But as professional interest in psychoanalysis—not all of it benevolent—grew apace, as Freud's upsetting ideas were being explored at psychiatrists' congresses, Freud aspired to enlarge the reach of psychoanalysis beyond its place of origin. Vienna, with its handful of followers, struck him as provincial, unsuitable as headquarters.

The first breakthrough came in 1906, when Jung, then principal psychiatrist at the renowned clinic Burghölzli in Zurich,
sent Freud an offprint. Freud responded promptly; a cordial
correspondence blossomed, and the friendship was cemented
by Jung's visit to Freud in early 1907. Freud was only fifty, vig-
orous and productive, but he had long brooded on himself as
aging and decrepit. He was seeking a successor who would
carry the psychoanalytic dispensation to later generations and
into a world larger than the Viennese, Jewish ambiance to
which psychoanalysis was then confined. Jung, a formidable
presence and energetic debater, was an inspired discovery: he
was not old, he was not Viennese, he was not Jewish. Jung was
prominent in the first international congress of psychoanalysts
at Salzburg in the spring of 1908, and was appointed, the following year, editor of a newly founded *Yearbook*. Freud,
delighted with Jung, anointed him his son, his crown prince—
accolades that Jung welcomed, indeed encouraged. Hence,
when the International Psychoanalytic Association was
founded in March 1910, in Nürnberg, Jung was Freud's logical,
inevitable, choice for president. Freud's Viennese adherents
saw their city displaced by Zurich as the center of psychoanalysis, and did not like it. A compromise was hammered out,
and for some time peace reigned in the Vienna Psychoanalytic
Society. But Adler was developing distinctive psychological
ideas, which featured aggressiveness over sexuality, and "organ
inferiority" as a dominant cause of neuroses. A split became
inevitable, and, in the summer of 1911, Adler and some of his

adherents resigned, leaving Freud and the Freudians in control of the Vienna society.

Freud was not without accolades. In September 1909, he had received an honorary doctorate at Clark University in Worces-ter, Massachusetts, as had Jung. But like Adler, Jung increas-ingly diverged from Freud's ideas. He had never been easy with the prominence Freud assigned to the sexual drive—libido. By early 1912, these reservations took a personal turn. In response, Ernest Jones, Freud's principal English lieutenant, formed a defensive secret band of like-minded analysts, the Committee. It consisted of himself, Freud, Sandor Ferenczi (a brilliant adherent from Budapest), the witty Viennese lawyer Hanns Sachs, the astute Berlin clinician and theorist Karl Abraham, and Freud's amanuensis, the autodidact Otto Rank. It seemed needed; by late 1912, the correspondence between Jung and Freud had grown acrimonious and in January 1914, Freud ter-minated his friendship with Jung. A split was only a matter of time; in the spring of 1914, Jung resigned from his powerful positions in the psychoanalytic movement.

⌐ The strains of psychoanalytic politics did not keep Freud from continuing his explorations of an impressive variety of topics. In 1913, he published an audacious, highly speculative venture into psychoanalytic prehistory, *Totem and Taboo*, which specified the moment that savages, in some dim, remote past, entered culture by murdering their father and acquiring guilt feelings. Then, in 1914, he published (anonymously) "The Moses of Michelan-gelo," uniting his admiration for Michelangelo's brooding sculpture with his powers of observation. In the same year, with an unsettling paper on narcissism, he subverted crucial aspects of psychoanalytic thought by throwing doubts upon his theory of drives—hitherto divided into erotic and egoistic.

But harrowing events on the world stage shouldered aside Freud's reassessment of psychoanalytic theory. On June 28, 1914, Austria's Archduke Francis Ferdinand and his consort were assassinated. Six weeks later, on August 4, Europe was at war. The first casualty for psychoanalysis was Freud's eventually best-known case history, "From the History of an Infantile Neurosis" ("Wolf Man"), written in the fall of 1914, but not published until 1918. Psychoanalytic activity almost ground to a halt. Many potential patients were at the front; most psychoanalysts were drafted into the medical corps; communications between "enemies" like Ernest Jones and Freud were severely truncated; psychoanalytic publications almost vanished; and congresses, the lifeblood of communication, were out of the question. For Freud, these were anxious times in other ways: all three of his sons were in the army, two of them almost daily in mortal danger.

Yet the war did not idle Freud's mind. Having too much time on his hands, he used it to good purpose. Work was a defense against brooding. Between March and July 1915, he wrote a dozen fundamental papers on metapsychology—on the unconscious, on repression, on melancholia; but he refused to gather them into the basic textbook he had planned. He published five of the papers between 1915 and 1917, and destroyed the rest. His enigmatic dissatisfaction with them hints at the discontent that had fueled his paper on narcissism. His map of the mind was inadequate to the evidence he had accumulated in his clinical experience. But he still lacked a satisfactory alternative. That would have to wait until after the war.

Another wartime activity, though more successful, gave Freud only modest pleasure: beginning in 1915, he delivered lectures at the university, published as a single volume in 1917 as *Introductory Lectures on Psycho-Analysis*. With the cunning of the born popularizer, Freud opened with a series on ordinary experiences, slips of the tongue, "unmotivated" forgetting, then turned to dreams and concluded with the technical topic, neuroses. Frequently reprinted and widely translated, these *Introductory Lectures* finally secured Freud a wide audience.

The war dragged on. Originally, somewhat to his surprise, an Austrian patriot, Freud wearied of the endless slaughter. He grew appalled at the chauvinism of intellectuals, the callousness of commanders, the stupidity of politicians. He had not yet fully acknowledged the theoretical significance of aggression, even though psychoanalysts had regularly encountered aggressiveness among their patients. But the war, beastly as it was, confirmed the skeptical psychoanalytic appraisal of human nature.

Signs of revived activity came shortly before the end of hostilities. In September 1918, for the first time since 1913, psychoanalysts from Germany and Austria-Hungary met in Budapest. Two months later, the war was over. To the family's immense relief, all of Freud's sons survived it. But the time for worry was far from over. The defeated powers were faced with revolution, drastically transformed from empires into republics, and saddled with stringent, vindictive peace treaties stripping them of territory and resources. Vienna was hungry, cold, desperate; food and fuel shortages produced deadly ailments—tuberculosis and influenza. In this stressful situation, Freud, who wasted no tears on the departed Hapsburg Empire, proved an energetic, imaginative manager. The portrait of Martha Freud shielding Herr Professor from domestic realities needs revision. Freud dispatched precise requests abroad to relatives, friends, associates, specifying what nourishment and clothing his family needed most, and how to send packages safely. Then, in January 1920, postwar misery struck home with deadly force: Freud's beloved second daughter Sophie, married and living in Hamburg, mother of two children, died in the influenza epidemic.

It has been plausibly argued that her death suggested the pessimistic drive theory that Freud now developed. Actually, he had virtually completed *Beyond the Pleasure Principle* (1920), which first announced Freud's theory of the death drive, the year before. Once Freud had adopted this construct, in which the forces of life, Eros, dramatically confront the forces of death, Thanatos, he found himself unable to think any other way. In 1923, in his classic study *The Ego and the Id*, he completed his revisions. He now proposed a "structural theory" of the mind, which visualizes the mind as divided into three distinct yet interacting agencies: the id (the wholly unconscious domain of the mind, consisting of the drives and of material later repressed), the ego (which is partly conscious and contains the defense mechanisms and the capacities to calculate, reason, and plan), and the super-ego (also only partly conscious, which harbors the conscience and, beyond that, unconscious feelings of guilt). This new scheme did not lead Freud to abandon his classic characterization of mental activity— emphasizing the distance of thoughts from awareness—as either conscious, or preconscious, or wholly unconscious. But he now made the decisive point that many of the mental operations of the ego, and of the super-ego as well, are inaccessible to direct introspection.

Meanwhile, the psychoanalytic movement was flourishing. Freud was becoming a household word, though he detested the sensationalized attention the popular press gave him. Better: in 1920, at the first postwar congress at The Hague, former "enemies" met as friends. Freud was accompanied by his daughter Anna, whom he was then analyzing and who joined the Vienna Psychoanalytic Society in 1922. In that year, the analysts convened in Berlin. It was the last congress Freud ever attended. In April 1923, he was operated on for a growth in his palate. While for months his doctors and closest associates pretended that the growth was benign, by September the truth was out: he had cancer. Severe operations followed in the fall. From then on Freud, compelled to wear a prosthesis, was rarely free of discomfort or pain.

But he never stopped working. While he had trouble speaking, he continued to analyze patients, many of them American physicians who came to Vienna as his "pupils" and returned to analyze in New York or Chicago. He continued to revise his theories. From the mid-1920s on, he wrote controversial papers on female sexuality, and, in 1926, *Inhibitions, Symptoms, and Anxiety*, which reversed his earlier thinking on anxiety, now treating it as a danger signal. Moreover, he wrote essays that found a relatively wide public: *The Future of an Illusion*, a convinced atheist's dissection of religion, in 1927, and, in 1930, *Civilization and Its Discontents*, a disillusioned look at modern civilization on the verge of catastrophe.

In 1933, that catastrophe came. On January 30, Hitler was appointed chancellor in Germany, and from then on Austrian Nazis, already active, increasingly intervened in politics. The old guard was disappearing: Karl Abraham had died prematurely in 1925; Sandor Ferenczi followed him in 1933. Freud's closest friends were gone. But Freud was unwilling to leave the Vienna he hated and loved: he was too old, he did not want to desert, and besides, the Nazis would never invade his country. On the morning of March 12, 1938, the Germans proved him wrong. As the Nazis marched in, a jubilant populace greeted them. Spontaneous anti-Semitic outrages surpassed anything Germans had witnessed after five years of Nazi rule. Late in March, Anna was summoned to Gestapo headquarters; while she was released unharmed, the trauma changed Freud's mind: he must emigrate. It took months to satisfy the Nazi government's extortions, but on June 4, Freud left for Paris, welcomed by his former analysand and loving disciple, Princess Marie Bonaparte. On June 6, Freud landed in London, preceded by most of his family, "to die in freedom."

Aged and ill, he kept on working. Freud's last completed book, *Moses and Monotheism*, irritated and dismayed his Jewish readers with its assertion that Moses had been an Egyptian: he ended life as he had lived it—a disturber of the peace. He died bravely on September 23, 1939, asking his physician for a lethal dose of morphine. Freud did not believe in personal immortality, but his work lives on.

TRANSLATOR'S NOTE
by James Strachey

(a) GERMAN EDITIONS:

1930   Vienna: Internationaler Psychoanalytischer Verlag. Pp. 136.

1931   2nd ed. (Reprint of 1st ed., with some additions.)

1934   G.S., 12, 29–114.

1948   G.W., 14, 421–506.

(b) ENGLISH TRANSLATION:

Civilization and Its Discontents

1930   London: Hogarth Press and Institute of Psycho-Analysis. New York: Cape and Smith. Pp. 144. (Tr. Joan Riviere.)

The present translation is based on that published in 1930.

THE FIRST CHAPTER of the German original was published slightly in advance of the rest of the book in *Psychoanal. Bewegung*, 1 (4), November–December, 1929. The fifth chapter appeared separately in the next issue of the same periodical, 2 (1), January–February, 1930. Two or three extra footnotes were included in the edition of 1931 and a new final sentence was added to the work. None of these additions appeared in the earlier version of the English translation.

Freud had finished *The Future of an Illusion* in the autumn of 1927. During the following two years, chiefly, no doubt, on account of his illness, he produced very little. But in the summer of 1929 he began writing another book, once more on a sociological subject. The first draft was finished by the end of July; the book was sent to the printers early in November and was actually published before the end of the year, though it carried the date '1930' on its title-page (Jones, 1957, 157–8).

The original title chosen for it by Freud was *'Das Unglück in der Kultur'* ('Unhappiness in Civilization'); but *'Unglück'* was later altered to *'Unbehagen'*—a word for which it was difficult to choose an English equivalent, though the French *'malaise'* might have served. Freud suggested *'Man's Discomfort in Civilization'* in a letter to his translator, Mrs. Riviere; but it was she herself who found the ideal solution of the difficulty in the title that was finally adopted.

BIBLIOGRAPHY

AND AUTHOR INDEX

LIST OF ABBREVIATIONS

G.S. = Freud, *Gesammelte Schriften* (12 vols.), Vienna, 1924–34

G.W. = Freud, *Gesammelte Werke* (18 vols.), London, from 1940

C.P. = Freud, *Collected Papers* (5 vols.), London, 1924–50

Standard Ed. = Freud, *Standard Edition* (24 vols.), New York, from 1953

TITLES OF BOOKS and periodicals are in italics; titles of papers are in inverted commas. Abbreviations are in accordance with the *World List of Scientific Periodicals* (London, 1952). Further abbreviations used in this volume will be found in the List above. Numerals in boldface refer to volumes; ordinary numerals refer to pages. The figures in parentheses at the end of each entry indicate the page or pages of this volume on which the work in question is mentioned. In the case of the Freud entries, the letters attached to the dates of publication are in accordance with the corresponding entries in the complete bibliography of Freud's writings included in the last volume of the *Standard Edition*.

For non-technical authors, and for technical authors where no specific work is mentioned, see the General Index.

AICHHORN, A. (1925) *Verwahrloste Jugend*, Vienna. (131) [*Trans.*: *Wayward Youth*, New York, 1935; London, 1936.]

ALEXANDER, F. (1927) *Die Psychoanalyse der Gesamtpersönlichkeit*, Vienna. (131)
[*Trans.*: *The Psychoanalysis of the Total Personality*, New York, 1930.]

ATKINSON, J. J. (1903) *Primal Law*, London. Included in A. Lang's *Social Origins*, London, 1903. (88)

BLEULER, E. (1913) 'Der Sexualwiderstand', *Jb. psychoan. psychopath. Forsch.*, 5, 442. (97)

BRANDES, G. (1896) *William Shakespeare*, Paris, Leipzig, Munich. (75)

DALY, C. D. (1927) 'Hindumythologie und Kastrationscomplex', *Imago*, 13, 145. (87)

FEDERN, P. (1926) 'Einige Variationen des Ichgefühls', *Int. Z. Psychoan.*, 12, 263. (39)
[*Trans.*: In *Ego Psychology and the Psychoses*, New York, 1952, 25.]
(1927) 'Narzissmus im Ichgefüge', *Int. Z. Psychoan.*, 13, 420. (39)
[*Trans.*: In *Ego Psychology and the Psychoses*, New York, 1952, 38.]

FERENCZI, S. (1913) 'Entwicklungsstufen des Wirklichkeitssinnes', *Int. Z. (ärztl.) Psychoanal.*, 1, 124. (39)
[*Trans.*: 'Stages in the Development of the Sense of Reality', *First Contributions to Psycho-Analysis*, London, 1952, Chap. VIII.

FREUD, S. (1895b) 'Über die Berechtigung von der Neurasthenie einen bestimmten Symptomenkomplex als "Angstneurose" abzutrennen', *G.S.* 1, 306; *G.W.*, 1, 315.
[*Trans.*: 'On the Grounds for Detaching a Particular Syndrome from Neurasthenia under the Description "Anxiety Neurosis"', *C.P.*, 1, 76; *Standard Ed.*, 3, 87.]

(1898*a*) 'Die Sexualität in der Ätiologie der Neurosen', *G.S.*, 1, 439;
G.W., 1, 491.
[*Trans.:* 'Sexuality in the Aetiology of the Neuroses', *C.P.*, 1, 220;
Standard Ed., 3, 261.]
(1900*a*) *Die Traumdeutung*, Vienna, *G.S.*, 2–3; *G.W.*, 2–3
[*Trans.: The Interpretation of Dreams*, London and New York, 1955;
Standard Ed., 4–5.]
(1901*a*) *Über den Traum*, Wiesbaden, *G.S.*, 3, 189; *G.W.*, 2–3, 643.
(135)
[*Trans.: On Dreams*, London and New York, 1951; *Standard Ed.*, 5,
633.]
(1901*b*) *Zur Psychopathologie des Alltagslebens*, Berlin, 1904. *G.S.*, 4, 3;
G.W., 4.
[*Trans.: The Psychopathology of Everyday Life; Standard Ed.*, 6.]
(1905*d*) *Drei Abhandlungen zur Sexualtheorie*, Vienna, *G.S.*, 5, 3; *G.W.*,
5, 29.
[*Trans.: Three Essays on the Theory of Sexuality*, London, 1949; *Standard
Ed.*, 7, 125.]
(1905*e* [1901]) 'Bruchstück einer Hysterie-Analyse', *G.S.*, 8, 3;
G.W., 5, 163. (74)
[*Trans.:* 'Fragment of an Analysis of a Case of Hysteria', *C.P.*, 3, 13;
Standard Ed., 7, 3.]
(1908 *b*) 'Charakter und Analerotik', *G.S.*, 5, 261; *G.W.*, 7, 203.
(83)
[*Trans.:* 'Character and Anal Erotism', *C.P.*, 2, 45; *Standard Ed.*, 9,
169.]
(1908*d*) 'Die "kulturelle" Sexualmoral und die moderne Nervosität',
G.S., 5, 143; *G.W.*, 7, 143.
[*Trans.:* '"Civilized" Sexual Morality and Modern Nervous Illness',
C.P., 2, 76; *Standard Ed.*, 9, 179.]

(1909b) 'Analyse der Phobie eines fünfjährigen Knaben', G.S., 8, 129; G.W., 7, 243.

[Trans.: 'Analysis of a Phobia in a Five-Year-Old Boy', C.P., 3, 149; Standard Ed., 10, 3.]

(1909d) 'Bemerkungen über einen Fall von Zwangsneurose', G.S., 8, 269; G.W., 7, 381.

[Trans.: 'Notes upon a Case of Obsessional Neurosis', C.P., 3, 293; Standard Ed., 10, 155.]

(1911b) 'Formulierungen über die zwei Prinzipien des psychischen Geschehens', G.S., 5, 409; G.W., 8, 230. (59)

[Trans.: 'Formulations on the Two Principles of Mental Functioning', C.P., 4, 13; Standard Ed., 12, 215.]

(1911c) 'Psychoanalytische Bemerkungen über einen autobiographisch beschriebenen Fall von Paranoia (Dementia Paranoides)', G.S., 8, 355; G.W., 8, 240.

[Trans.: 'Psycho-Analytic Notes on an Autobiographical Account of a Case of Paranoia (Dementia Paranoides)', C.P., 3, 387; Standard Ed., 12, 3.]

(1912d) 'Über die allgemeinste Erniedrigung des Liebeslebens', G.S., 5, 198; G.W., 8, 78.

[Trans.: 'On the Universal Tendency to Debasement in the Sphere of Love', C.P., 4, 203; Standard Ed., 11, 179.]

(1912–13) Totem und Tabu, Vienna, 1913. G.S., 10, 3; G.W., 9. (88, 132, 140)

[Trans.: Totem and Taboo, London, 1950; New York, 1952; Standard Ed., 13, 1.]

(1913f) 'Das Motiv der Kästchenwahl', G.S., 10, 243; G.W., 10, 244. (75)

[Trans.: 'The Theme of the Three Caskets', C.P., 4, 244; Standard Ed., 12, 291.]

(1915b) 'Zeitgemässes über Krieg und Tod', G.S., 10, 315; G.W., 10, 324.

[Trans.: 'Thoughts for the Times on War and Death', C.P., 4, 288, Standard Ed., 14, 275.]

(1915c) 'Triebe und Triebschicksale', G.S., 5, 443; G.W., 10, 210.

[Trans.: 'Instincts and their Vicissitudes', C.P., 4, 60; Standard Ed., 14, 143.]

(1915f) 'Mitteilung eines der psychoanalytischen Theorie widersprechenden Falles von Paranoia', G.S., 5, 288; G.W., 10, 243.

[Trans: 'A Case of Paranoia Running Counter to the Psycho-Analytic Theory of the Disease', C.P., 2, 150; Standard Ed., 14, 263.])

(1916–17) Vorlesungen zur Einführung in die Psychoanalyse, Vienna. G.S., 7; G.W., 11. (59)

[Trans · Introductory Lectures on Psycho Analysis, London, 1929 (A General Introduction to Psychoanalysis, New York, 1935), Standard Ed, 15–16.]

(1918a) 'Das Tabu der Virginität', G.S., 5, 212; G.W., 12, 161.

[Trans.: 'The Taboo of Virginity', C.P., 4, 217; Standard Ed., 11, 193.]

(1920g) Jenseits des Lustprinzips, Vienna, G.S., 6, 191; G.W., 13, 3. (113)

[Trans.: Beyond the Pleasure Principle, London, 1961; Standard Ed., 18, 3.]

(1921c) Massenpsychologie und Ich-Analyse, Vienna. G.S., 6, 261; G.W., 13, 73. (110)

[Trans.: Group Psychology and the Analysis of the Ego, London, 1959; New York, 1960; Standard Ed., 18, 67.]

(1923b) Das Ich und das Es, Vienna. G.S., 6, 353; G.W., 13, 237.

[Trans.: The Ego and the Id, New York, 1961; Standard Ed., 19, 3.]

(1924c) 'Das ökonomische Problem des Masochismus', G.S., 5, 374; G.W., 13, 371. (106)

[*Trans.:* 'The Economic Problem of Masochism', *C.P.,* 2, 255; *Standard Ed.,* 19, 157.]

(1925*e*) 'Die Widerstände gegen die Psychoanalyse', *G.S.,* 11, 224; *G.W.,* 14, 99.

[*Trans.:* 'The Resistances to Psycho-Analysis', *C.P.,* 5, 163; *Standard Ed.,* 19, 213.]

(1925*b*) 'Die Verneinung', *G.S.,* 11, 3; *G.W.,* 14, 11.

[*Trans.:* 'Negation', *C.P.,* 5, 181; *Standard Ed.,* 19, 235.]

(1926*d*) *Hemmung, Symptom und Angst,* Vienna., *G.S.,* 11, 23; *G.W.,* 14, 113.

[*Trans.: Inhibitions, Symptoms and Anxiety,* London, 1960 (*The Problem of Anxiety,* New York, 1936); *Standard Ed.,* 20, 77.]

(1926*e*) *Die Frage der Laienanalyse,* Vienna. *G.S.,* 11, 307; *G.W.,* 14, 209. (63)

[*Trans.: The Question of Lay Analysis,* London, 1947, New York, 1950; *Standard Ed.,* 20, 179.]

(1927*c*) *Die Zukunft einer Illusion,* Vienna., *G.S.,* 11, 411; *G.W.,* 14, 325. (36, 49, 73, 79, 140, 152)

[*Trans.: The Future of an Illusion,* London and New York, 1928; *Standard Ed.,* 21, 3.]

(1930*a*) *Das Unbehagen in der Kultur,* Vienna. *G.S.,* 12, 29; *G.W.,* 14, 421.

[*Trans.: Civilization and Its Discontents,* London, 1930, New York, 1962; *Standard Ed.,* 21, 59.]

(1931*a*) 'Über libidinöse Typen', *G.S.,* 12, 115; *G.W.,* 14, 509.

[*Trans.:* 'Libidinal Types', *C.P.,* 5, 247; *Standard Ed.,* 21, 215.]

(1932*a*) 'Zur Gewinnung des Feuers', *G.S.,* 12, 141; *G.W.,* 16, 3. (73–74)

[*Trans.:* 'The Acquisition and Control of Fire', *C.P.,* 5, 288; *Standard Ed.,* 22.]

(1933*a*) *Neue Folge der Vorlesungen zur Einführung in die Psychoanalyse,* Vienna. G.S., 12, 151; G.W., 15, 207.

[*Trans.: New Introductory Lectures on Psycho-Analysis,* London and New York, 1933; *Standard Ed.,* 22.]

(1933*b*) *Warum Krieg?,* G.S., 12, 349; G.W., 16, 13. (85)

[*Trans.: Why War?,* C.P., 5, 273; *Standard Ed.,* 22.]

(1937c) 'Die endliche und die unendliche Analyse', G.W., 16, 59.

[*Trans.:* 'Analysis Terminable and Interminable', C.P., 5, 316; *Standard Ed.,* 23.]

(1939*a* [1937–39]) *Der Mann Moses und die monotheistische Religion,* G.W., 16, 103. (126)

[*Trans.: Moses and Monotheism,* London and New York, 1939; *Standard Ed.,* 23.]

(1940*a* [1938]) *Abriss der Psychoanalyse,* G.W., 17, 67.

[*Trans.: An Outline of Psycho-Analysis,* London and New York, 1949; *Standard Ed.* 23.]

(1950*a* [1887–1902]) *Aus den Anfängen der Psychoanalyse,* London. Includes 'Entwurf einer Psychologie' (1895). (125)

[*Trans.: The Origins of Psycho-Analysis,* London and New York, 1954. (Partly, including 'A Project for a Scientific Psychology', in *Standard Ed.,* 1.)]

JONES, E. (1918) 'Anal-Erotic Character Traits', *J. abnorm. Psychol.,* 13, 261; *Papers on Psycho-Analysis,* London and New York, 1918 (2nd ed.), Chap. XL. (83)

(1957) *Sigmund Freud: Life and Work,* Vol. 3, London and New York. (Page references are to the English edition.)

RICKMAN, J. (ed.) (1939) *Civilization, War and Death: Selections from Three Works by Sigmund Freud,* London.

GENERAL INDEX

This index includes the names of non-technical authors. It also includes the names of technical authors where no reference is made in the text to specific works. For references to specific technical works, the Bibliography should be consulted.